THE OFFICIAL SORORITY HANDBOOK™

THE OFFICIAL SORORITY HANDBOOK™

Kirsten McLean

This book was printed in the United States of America.

To order additional copies of this book, contact:
Xlibris Corporation
1-888-795-4274
www.Xlibris.com
Orders@Xlibris.com
20276

CONTENTS

*This book is dedicated with love to
my husband and my children.*

-Foreword-

The process of joining a college sorority is secretive and mysterious with its rituals, traditions and ceremonies. The Official Sorority Handbook demystifies the process of joining a college sorority. Although sororities are not right for everyone, they do serve a purpose.

Sororities are not just about frat parties. Sororities provide consistency and are a small village within a large college/university campus. Sororities can inspire you to achieve your best self by promoting high scholarship, good citizenship, leadership, service to others and personal development.

Read on and decide whether you want to participate in the sorority Recruitment process when you go off to college!

OFF TO COLLEGE YOU GO!

Congratulations, you are off to college! Just when you complete your college entrance exams, college applications, scholarship and financial aid requests, it's time to consider whether you want to join a sorority during your freshman year in college.

Sororities choose new members through a mutual selection process called "Recruitment" (formerly known as "Rush"). Sorority Recruitment is a formal schedule of events organized by sororities to meet prospective sorority members.

Most college sorority Recruitment occurs in the fall, but some colleges have "deferred Recruitment" which occurs during the spring. Many sororities prohibit college juniors from pledging a sorority, so the decision to join a sorority must occur before you begin college or during your first year at college.

Joining a sorority can be a nerve racking and anxiety provoking process. Going off to a large college, living in a dorm and going through Recruitment to join a sorority is an exciting time. Nevertheless, going through Recruitment can also be a painful experience if you are not invited to join the sorority of your choice or you do not receive an offer to join any sorority.

The good news is if you prepare for Recruitment in the same manner you prepare for enrolling in college, you increase the chances of joining the sorority of your choice. The same skills you use to investigate and apply to sororities will help you later in life when you are investigating and applying for jobs.

Remember, each of us is unique. This Handbook will help you navigate the sorority system; however, the best advice is to be true to yourself by acting like you!

WANT TO JOIN A SORORITY?

If you are considering joining a sorority during your freshman year in college, ask yourself what kind of sorority would you like to join? Not all sororities are the same—some sororities are "traditional" and others are "non-traditional".

Generally speaking, the non-traditional sororities are religious or multi-cultural based. African-American sororities, Christian sororities, Jewish sororities, Military Sororities, Native American sororities, Asian-American sororities, and Latina sororities are located on many college campuses.

Regardless of whether you are interested in joining a traditional or non-traditional sorority, all sororities encourage a bond of sisterhood, require a minimum grade point average, encourage campus leadership, plan activities and serve a philanthropic purpose. Also, let us not forget that sororities are well known for planning social events throughout the year.

Before we learn more, we need to start with the basics!

LESSON 1

THE GREEK ALPHABET

All sororities have Greek names. Therefore, your first lesson to learn before deciding whether you even want to join a sorority is to learn the Greek alphabet! After all, you must be able to state a sorority's name properly. The Greek alphabet begins with A (alpha) and ends with Ω (omega). The Greek alphabet (with phonetic pronunciation) is in the proper order as follows:

A	Alpha (al-fah)
B	Beta (bay-tah)
Γ	Gamma (gam-ah)
Δ	Delta (del-ta)
E	Epsilon (ep-si-lon)
Z	Zeta (zay-tah)
H	Eta (ay-tah)
Θ	Theta (thay-tah)
I	Iota (eye-o-tah)
K	Kappa (cap-pah)
Λ	Lamda (lamb-dah)
M	Mu (mew)
I	Nu (new)
Ξ	Xi (zie)
O	Omicron (om-e-cron)
Π	Pi (pie)
P	Rho (roe)
Σ	Sigma (sig-mah)
T	Tau (taw)

Υ	Upsilon (up-si-lon)
Φ	Phi (fie)
Χ	Chi (kie)
Ψ	Psi (sigh)
Ω	Omega (oh-may-gah)

Now that you have learned the Greek alphabet, you will not only be able to identify a sorority house name, you can identify a fraternity house too!

LESSON 2

COLLEGE ACADEMICS

All sororities require minimum grade point averages for its active members. Most colleges require that each new sorority member maintain a specific number of class credit hours and maintain a minimum grade point average prior to initiation.

Unfortunately, study time is not allocated during the designated Recruitment period, so you must plan and organize your homework time efficiently during the Recruitment process.

Most, if not all, sororities promote academic excellence. Your scholastic endeavors are encouraged and often publicly recognized. You are expected to attend all of your classes; maintain a full course load; and, exceed a minimum grade point average.

Some sororities may require you to study for a certain number of hours per week at the sorority house. Sorority sisters are willing to tutor you or develop programs that will assist you in your schoolwork.

Fortunately, sororities allocate study time programs during the "Pledge" term (the period of time after you have accepted a sorority's bid, but you have not been initiated) and during active membership. And, although joining a sorority takes time away from studying, many campuses report that sorority grade point averages, overall, are higher than non-sorority grade point averages.

LESSON 3

THE SORORITY ADVANTAGE

While Sororities are not right for everyone, the majority of women who have joined sororities have found them to be personally fulfilling both during and after their college "careers." Consider the following when evaluating whether to join a sorority:

- **Sisterhood & Friendship**

  If you attend a large university or college, joining a sorority creates a smaller community within a large campus.

  As a sorority member or pledge, you immediately have a group of people who may have similar interests as you. This does not mean all those in a sorority will be your friends or even act friendly toward you, but it does provide a place you can call home away from your home.

  Sororities encourage bonding among its members by nurturing sisterhood and friendship through its activities.

- **Housing & Meals**

  Some campuses have housing shortages and joining a sorority may guarantee you housing near campus.

  Further, if you cannot cook, do not like to cook, or you want to improve from the taste of dorm food, many sororities provide three hot meals per day (with the exception of Sunday night meals). As an added bonus, many sororities have busboys (usually fraternity boys) that serve you a sit-down meal each evening. Did I also mention, you are served a full course meal which includes dessert and the busboys do the dishes?

• **Laundry & Cleaning Services**

Many sororities have laundry and cleaning services available. Imagine having all of your laundry and cleaning taken care of during your college years!

• **Parking**

Sororities may have parking spaces that allow you to keep a car near campus. Campus parking is typically at a premium. Many campuses forbid students from bringing cars to campus unless you are one of the lucky few that won a slot in a college lottery or you have access to an assigned parking spot at a sorority.

• **Social Events**

Sororities have designated social occasions and traditions (e.g. Friday night pizza nights) that allow you outlets from studying. Sororities maintain a calendar of events that range from fraternity parties, formal parties, Greek week events, sporting events, mixers, casuals, date dashes, chapter events, chapter retreats, dinner dances, parent weekends, Recruitment parties, and date nights, to athletic pre-game parties.

Sororities encourage and offer a wide variety of activities that you may not otherwise experience (e.g. organized intramural sports, community activities, campus activities, and philanthropic activities).

Sororities typically sit together at sporting events, cultural events, and school events. Thus, you always have someone you know (or at least recognize) at events where you may otherwise feel strange.

- **Study Facilities**

  Sororities are founded on high academic achievement and encourage study groups to meet in the sorority house study area. Many sororities have state of the art technology and office spaces set up so you do not need to leave the sorority house to access university computers, make photocopies, or send facsimiles.

- **Networking/Mentoring Programs**

  Sororities have unlimited access to others in your field of study through alumnae organizations. Alumnae provide an excellent resource of information and have mentor programs available.

  Once you join a sorority, you create a lifelong association that can be used later for networking on a professional basis or provide an avenue to meet others through alumnae organizations if you move to a different community after college graduation.

  Pledging a sorority proves worthwhile beyond graduation. The latest Forbes Super 500 list indicates that many chief executives on America's largest corporations were members of college "Greek systems" (i.e. a member of a sorority or a fraternity). The Forbes article suggests that the same social skills used to get into the Greek system is advantageous by building connections and establishing networking connections for its members.

- **Leadership Skills**

  Sororities are active in academic, political, and social activities on college campuses. Sorority members often hold leadership positions to carry out these activities, further enhancing their college experience.

  Sororities have leadership training programs for its officers and can open doors to community and campus organizations by providing "service to others".

  You'll find sororities often dedicate themselves to volunteerism by donating time to philanthropic events and sponsoring fundraisers to raise money for worthy causes (Yes, sororities are preparing you to join a Junior League after graduating from college. After all, sororities and the Junior League focus on developing and empowering women leaders to increase the impact that people make in their communities.)

LESSON 4

THE SORORITY DISADVANTAGE

Joining a sorority is not all about frat parties, fun, and games. Sororities have financial commitments, time commitments, moral commitments, and responsibilities that go along with being a member. Consider the following when evaluating whether to join a sorority:

- **Financial Commitments**

  Sororities require social dues and obligations. Most sororities have additional one-time pledging dues, initiation fees, badge fees, and national enrollment fees. Specific financial information may be obtained from individual sorority chapters.

  Many sororities have payment plans or need-based scholarship programs available to assist with the financial commitment of sorority membership and housing costs. Nevertheless, these funds may be limited. Thus, an important consideration in deciding whether to join a sorority is whether you can meet the financial responsibilities of membership dues, meal fees, housing costs, yearly fees, and extra expenses of t-shirts, pictures, jewelry, social events, party favors etc.

- **Time Commitments**

  Sororities have time commitments that go along with being

a member. Sororities require its members to participate in mandatory events—(e.g. yearly Recruitment, monthly meetings, committee groups, volunteer service, retreats, and designated campus events.)

Additionally, many sororities require its members to be involved in activities outside of the sorority. Therefore, before you join a sorority, consider whether you have the maturity not to overextend yourself. You need to have the ability to organize your time efficiently and wisely between your sorority commitments, your school commitments and all of your other activities.

If you are entering a demanding field of study, it may be difficult to juggle the mandatory time commitments required by the sorority with a demanding school schedule.

- **Housing & Meal Obligations**

  Sororities may have mandatory housing arrangements that will not allow its members to live out of the sorority house until an active member's senior year in college. Even if you are a senior, you may have to enter the sorority's lottery system to see if you can live outside of the house.

  Sororities may assess rent, food and laundry fees that may be at a higher rate than other alternative campus housing.

  Sororities may require meal plans with mandatory eating times. If you cannot schedule your school classes around the eating times, you may not have access to a meal. Further, you may not be able to attend a meal late or leave a meal early unless you receive permission from the "House Mother" (i.e. the woman who manages the sorority house and its meals).

- **Stereotypes & Moral Commitments**

  Sorority members are stereotyped from others outside the sorority system.

  Sorority members require "moral commitments" of supporting sorority sisters and upholding the sorority's standards.

- **Social Obligations**

  Designated sorority chairpersons decide all social arrangements for the sorority house members. If you do not like what social arrangements have been scheduled, you may be obligated to attend a specific number of events.

- **Limits on Visitors**

  Sororities may limit the time and location you can receive visitors. Overnight guests (especially those of the opposite sex) may be forbidden. Thus, if you have a brother or a boyfriend that attends a different college and is planning on "crashing" at your place for the weekend, they may not be permitted to do so in most (if not all) sororities.

- **Hazing**

  Sorority members may be subjected to hazing. Hazing is defined as doing things that are against your will, violate you, or could cause you imminent harm. [*See* "Lesson 22: Hazing & Personal Safety" in this Handbook for an in-depth discussion of this important topic.]

LESSON 5

ARE YOU THE SORORITY TYPE?

What is the sorority type? Whatever comes to mind—let it go! Sorority girls are as individual and different as any two or more girls anywhere! Yes, you'll find sorority girls who wear designer clothes and carry designer handbags. Many look the part of the country club set. And yes, you'll also find sorority girls who were high school homecoming queens, student council presidents and cheerleaders.

Nevertheless, each sorority chapter is comprised of many different females with different qualities and attributes. It is difficult to determine exactly what sororities are looking for in a new member. Sorority members differ house-by-house and campus-by-campus from year-to-year. The members at a Chi Omega house at the University of Michigan may be very different than the members at the Chi Omega house at the University of Texas.

Sororities continue to maintain a reputation for being a breeding ground of young women going off to college to earn a "MRS." degree by marrying a wealthy fraternity boy. And although this can (and frequently does) happen, most young women who join sororities are the future leaders of tomorrow.

Sororities are comprised of future doctors, attorneys, accountants, artists, CEOs, bankers, engineers, judges, teachers, journalists, stock brokers, homemakers, teachers, artists, non-profit officers, actors and anything else a person dreams of becoming.

Do not believe everything you hear about people in a specific sorority. On a national level, sororities seem to have developed reputations and stereotypes; but, the best source of information is embodied in the members of a particular sorority chapter. That being said, the only opinion that counts is yours. Do not be influenced by someone else's perceptions or decisions.

Some of the reputations of sororities on your college campus may or may not be true. Always keep an open mind when going through Recruitment. Only you can decide if a particular sorority is right for you!

Sororities strive for a well-balanced and diverse pledge class. Each of us is unique and each sorority is unique. Sororities look for a variety of members. You do not need to be the life of a party to be a member of a sorority. If you are shy, it is okay. Good sororities will honor and respect "genuineness."

A perfect sorority "type" does not exist. If you want to join a sorority, chances are that you will find a sorority house that will seem like a perfect match for you!

LESSON 6

RECRUITMENT / RUSH—WHAT IS IT?

Recruitment is a term used to describe the entire process of joining a sorority. Essentially, Recruitment is a time period designated by your college "Greek Life Office" (which may also be called Student Affairs, Multi-Cultural Greek Council, Panhellenic Office, Panhellenic Council, Greek Relations Office, Sorority & Fraternity Relations or Greek Life Center). From hereon, "Greek Life Office" will be used generically to reference the college's supporting administrative office of sorority and fraternity affairs.

Recruitment allows sororities and new members to choose each other through a mutual selection process. The Recruitment process allows for sorority members to meet prospective young women to become members of their sorority through carefully planned and scheduled activities. In order to become a member of a sorority, you must go through the Recruitment process.

Typically, there are two types of Recruitment—Formal Recruitment and Informal Recruitment. Formal Recruitment is an organized and structured set of activities that consist of several rounds of parties. The parties allow you to get acquainted with sorority life. Conversely, Informal Recruitment has no schedules. The meeting times are scheduled directly between the sorority and each potential member.

The reason for having a Formal Recruitment process is that it ensures that each sorority has equal opportunities for membership

Recruitment within the Greek life system. Further, a Formal Recruitment process allows each Potential New Member ("Rushee") every opportunity to become acquainted with all of the sororities (or as many as possible) in order to make an informed decision when deciding on first and second choices for sorority membership.

Unfortunately, not everyone going through the Recruitment process will be given an invitation to join a sorority. Each sorority has a maximum number of women that it may accept into its sorority each year. The competition may be tight depending on how many women want to get into a particular sorority chapter.

As you will learn in "Behind the Scenes," it is not a reflection of you if you do not receive an invitation to join a sorority. Truly, whether you join a sorority or not is based on so many factors that are not within your control (e.g. whether you have met a lot of people in the sorority; whether these people are speaking up for you during the voting process; whether these people are liked in the sorority etc.). Let me repeat—whether or not you are given an invitation to join a sorority involve factors *outside* of your control. Thus, all you can do is be yourself and hope for the best!

LESSON 7

RECRUITMENT / RUSH—WHEN IS IT?

Sorority Recruitment is a formal process for members of a sorority to meet potential members to join the sorority. Recruitment is different at every college campus.

Most colleges and universities conduct Formal Recruitment in the beginning of the fall semester, but you most contact your campus to obtain the actual Recruitment dates as some campuses begin and complete its Recruitment weeks before the official school year begins.

Once you have been accepted to a college and chosen a college to attend, contact your college's Greek Life Office, Admission Office, or Local Alumnae Chapter to obtain information on the sorority Recruitment process.

If you are considering joining a sorority, it is imperative that you do the following to sign up for Recruitment:

- **DURING FEBRUARY/MARCH OF YOUR SENIOR YEAR IN HIGH SCHOOL:**

  1. Ask your school guidance counselor if college sorority "Information Nights" are being held locally. Sorority alumnae associations hold Information Nights in large metropolitan areas to provide high school girls and their parents with information regarding sororities and

assist with the reference process. Specifically, alumnae associations provide valuable information regarding the Recruitment process and information about sororities on a national level.

2. Sign up for the "Information Night" meeting and encourage your parents to attend. You can ask any questions about sororities and the selection process.

3. Develop a "resume" of your accomplishments that lists your: job history (if any); high school activities (i.e. clubs, offices, sports); awards or honors; community/ volunteer activities; and any talents, hobbies or interests that you have.

4. Attend "Information Night" and pick-up an "Information Form" at the meeting. Information Forms are preliminary forms used by Sororities in alumnae associations. The alumnae association sororities' mail completed Information Forms to college sororities around the country. This notifies sororities at your college campus that you are considering joining a sorority when you enter college.

5. Complete your Information Form and return before the stated deadline (usually in mid-June).

6. After completing your Information Form, attach a "resume" of your accomplishments and an informal photograph of you to the form. Although attaching a photograph is considered optional, it is highly recommended that you do so. Sororities receive packets of information and begin associating names and faces long before the Recruitment parties begin.

Presumably, the Information Form, photograph, and resume of your accomplishments will give you a head start in the Recruitment process by helping you stand out in the crowd!

7. Visit your University's Internet site to obtain

information about the Formal Recruitment process. Specifically, request information regarding the Recruitment process. You may be able to register for Recruitment on-line. If the Internet site does not contain sorority Recruitment information, contact your university's Greek Life Office.

- **DURING JUNE OF YOUR SENIOR YEAR IN HIGH SCHOOL OR IMMEDIATELY FOLLOWING HIGH SCHOOL GRADUATION:**

    1. Obtain paperwork from your college to register for the Formal Recruitment process. Even if you completed "Information Forms" from sorority alumnae associations, you must register with your college for sorority Recruitment.
    2. Write the Recruitment dates on your calendar. Make plans to attend all Recruitment parties. You cannot join a sorority unless you go through the Recruitment process.
    3. Pay Recruitment registration fees. Recruitment fees cover administration expenses associated with processing your paperwork, distributing Recruitment materials, and providing meals and beverages.
    4. Complete Recruitment paperwork before the school year begins.
    5. Submit Recruitment paperwork to the proper college office before the Recruitment submission deadline.
    6. Provide copies of your high school transcripts, if requested.
    7. Ask friends, neighbors, mothers, and grandmothers who were members of college sororities to write "Letters of Reference" (formerly referred to as "Recommendations") on your behalf. You are not required to find your own Letters of Reference, but these letters are helpful as some sororities only invite you back to the 2nd round events if

you have a reference letter on file. Generally, sororities must receive reference letters by late-July to mid-August.

Thus, you must begin asking others to write letters of reference for you in June to allow alumnae time to obtain the proper forms without missing a deadline. [*See* "Lesson 11: Reference Letters & Legacies" in this Handbook for an in-depth discussion on this topic.]

8. Verify whether you can meet the financial obligations of joining a sorority—social dues, housing and food expenses (if you are required to live in the sorority house).
9. If your college campus begins Recruitment *before* the official school year begins, make a hotel reservation because the dorms/residence halls will not be open.
10. Request a refund, if it is necessary to cancel your Recruitment registration. You must withdraw and request a refund before your college's designated deadline.

LESSON 8

FORMAL RECRUITMENT/RUSH

Formal Recruitment is an organized schedule through which prospective members (sometimes referred to as "Potential New Members" or "Rushees") visit sorority houses.

"Potential New Members" are given an opportunity to become familiar with all facets of sorority life through carefully planned and scheduled activities. The trend is toward a "no-frills" Recruitment. Unlike your mother's or grandmother's experience, less emphasis is on skits and musical revues and more emphasis is on conversation.

Recruitment is often a very emotional time. You may experience emotions ranging from complete joy to total disappointment.

Recruitment schedules, the number of Recruitment events, and Recruitment rules vary greatly by college. Some colleges may have the Recruitment process over a few days to a few weeks while others may have it longer. Some colleges have multiple visits (sometimes referred to as "sets" or "events") while others have a few.

Generally, you will have three rounds of Recruitment parties (sometimes referred to as "visits") before you select your top choices. Your schedule of Recruitment parties is reduced from round to round. Following the final Recruitment party, you will select your top sorority choices. These last parties are often referred to as

"Preferential Rounds" (or may be referred to as "Final Desserts", "Final Rounds", or "Prefs").

Notwithstanding of the number of Recruitment events scheduled at your campus, you will attend a whirlwind of parties (this explains why Recruitment was formerly known as "Rush"). The Recruitment parties allow time for you and active sorority women to get to know one another before deciding on a sorority to join.

1.   The Recruitment Group

During Formal Recruitment, Potential New Members are divided into Recruitment Groups. The groups may vary in size. Normally, the Recruitment Groups are divided by a person's last name, but the groups may be divided by residence hall/dorm, social security number, date of Recruitment application submission etc.

2.   The Recruitment Counselor

The Greek Life Office assigns each Recruitment Group to a Recruitment Counselor (also called "Rho Chi" or "RC"). A Recruitment Counselor is trained to be your counselor and guide through the Recruitment process.

A Recruitment Counselor ensures that you attend each house on time; the Recruitment rules are obeyed; and the Formal Recruitment process runs smoothly. Most importantly, the Recruitment Counselor knows the location of each of the sororities and she will make sure that you arrive at each house on time.

Never be afraid to ask your Recruitment Counselor questions, as you must be able to make informed decisions when choosing what sorority you would like to join. However, asking questions of the Recruitment Counselor and inquiring about the Recruitment process is very different than discussing your opinion of the different sororities.

Generally, you should not discuss your opinion about any of the sororities in front of a Recruitment Counselor. Your Recruitment Counselor is a member of one of the sororities. Your Recruitment Counselor is not able to reveal to you which sorority she is a member of until Formal Recruitment officially ends.

A Recruitment Counselor is not allowed to vote during the Formal Recruitment process. She is prohibited from discussing any information about the Potential New Members assigned to her Recruitment group to members of her sorority. Nevertheless, you should exercise good judgment and not discuss anything negative about any sorority with the Recruitment Counselor. Recruitment Counselors may talk about their Recruitment groups with other members of their sororities.

3. The "First Visit"/"Round One"/"First Set"/ "Ice Water Teas"/"Open House"

At some college campuses, you will visit *all* of the sororities on the "First Visit". At "Invitation Only" college campuses, you may only visit the sorority houses that invite you to the "First Visit".

If you are attending college in the south (or a college with a large number of sorority houses), it is likely that you will only be allowed to visit the sorority houses that have reviewed your Recruitment application in the summer and have personally extended an invitation for Formal Recruitment. Thus, you need to determine before Recruitment whether your college campus visits every sorority house on the first visit or whether it is by invitation only.

During the first round of the Formal Recruitment process, you will spend a specified amount of time at each sorority. The first round is allocated the shortest amount of time to spend at each sorority.

At each sorority, you will typically shake the hand of its members and introduce yourself. The Sorority President, Recruitment Chairperson or other designated members of the sorority will welcome you to their house and discuss what it is like to be a member of that particular sorority.

Some sororities may show videos of a day in the life of the sorority members; others may discuss the sorority calendar for the year etc. Sorority house tours may be given, if allowed by your college's Greek Life Office Recruitment rules.

Typically, you will meet at least three active sorority members during the first designated time period. Although, in some sorority houses you may meet only a few sorority members and at other sorority houses you may meet many sorority members.

Potential New Members and active sorority members make small talk and are "sizing" each other up on whether or not a particular sorority is a "good fit." You will be asked a lot of questions about yourself (e.g. Where are you from? What is your intended major? What did you do last summer? What activities do you like? Where are you living?).

You will get tired of repeating yourself, but try and remember that each sorority house is a new group of sorority sisters that wants to get the chance to meet you. Also, do not be afraid to ask questions. You can ask them the same questions that they ask you or come up with your own questions. For a list of suggested questions, refer to "Lesson 16: The Art of Conversation" in this Handbook.

Do not believe that the sorority selection process is one sided. Recruitment is a mutual selection process. As a Potential New Member, you influence this process as well. Members of sororities are disappointed when Potential New Members decline to accept its invitations for second and third visits.

Last, some colleges allow informal visits after the first round of

Formal Recruitment. The informal visits are a chance for you to visit the houses you liked and spend additional time meeting the other sorority members. It is a great chance for you to find out additional information without having a designated time limit at each house.

Inquire whether your college permits informal visits between scheduled Recruitment parties. If your college allows informal visits, take this opportunity to learn more about the sororities so you can better make an informed decision on Preference Day.

4.   The "Second Visit"/ "Round Two"/ "Second Set"/"InvitationalRound"

After the first round of sorority visits, the entire sorority meets to discuss the first round of visits. The sorority's Recruitment Chairperson states your name and asks its active sorority members to vote on whether you should be invited back to the sorority for the next set of events. Only the sorority members that have met you are allowed to vote.

Generally, sororities use three criteria when voting:

1. Scholarship (your grades);
2. Extracurricular Activities; and,
3. Personality.

After the vote, sororities assign you a score and rank all Potential New Members from the highest score to the lowest score on a tabulation sheet. The tabulation sheet ranking determines whether you are invited back to the sorority for a second visit. The tabulation sheet is given to the Greek Life Office. The Greek Life Office enters this information into a computer system. Once all of the information is entered, the Greek Life Office prints you a report of those sororities that have invited you back for a second round of parties.

As a Potential New Member, you may be told by the Greek Life Office that you can choose to go back to all of the houses that invited you back for a "Second Visit" or you may be asked to pick your top selections. (Note: colleges that ask you to pick your top selections place a limit on the number of selections that you can make for your Second Visit.)

Once you have made your selections, you return your sheet to the Greek Life Office. The Greek Life Office enters your selections into its computer system. Once all the Potential New Members have submitted their selections, the Greek Life Office runs a report for each Potential New Member designating the sorority and time period for each second round of parties.

Again, if you attend a college campus that handles sorority Recruitment by invitation only, you are hand delivered an invitation to the second event by the specific sorority.

The second rounds of parties are similar to the first round, but the parties are scheduled for a longer period of time. This longer time period allows you to become better acquainted with the sorority house. Basically, the longer time period gives you and sororities' additional time to learn more about each other.

Many times the sororities provide informative entertainment to learn more about the sorority. You may see a skit, a slide show, or listen to a group sing. Generally, you are told about the sorority's philanthropies and sisterhood events. Try to relax during the entertainment. You will find that some sorority members are more talented than others. The good news is that they are having fun despite the fact that they may never perform professionally on Broadway!

Frequently, active sorority members take you around the sorority house and introduce you to other active sorority members. Take advantage of this opportunity by keeping your eyes and ears open.

The more you can learn the better off you will be when making an informed decision for eliminating sorority houses at the end of each round of Recruitment.

5.   The "Third Visit"/"Round Three"/"Third Sets"/ "Preference Parties"/"Pref Parties"/ "Final Desserts"

After the Second Visit, the sorority's Recruitment Chairman states your name and asks the active sorority members that met you during the Recruitment party to vote on whether you should be invited back to the sorority for a third and final visit.

After the vote, sororities assign a score and rank the Potential New Members from the highest score to lowest score on a tabulation sheet. The tabulation sheet determines whether you are invited back to the sorority for the "Third Visit". The tabulation sheet is given to the Greek Life Office where the information is entered into a computer system. Once all of the information is entered, the Greek Life Office prints a report of those sororities that invited you back for a third round of parties. The third round of parties is often called "Preference Parties."

Any sorority that invites you to the final round/"preferential party" is considering you for membership. At most colleges, you are allowed to attend 2 or 3 different sorority houses for the final preference event.

As a Potential New Member, you may be told by the Greek Life Office that you can choose to go back to all of the houses that invited you back or you may be asked to pick your top selections. (Note: colleges that ask you to pick your top selections will place a limit on the number of selections.)

Once you have made your decisions, return your sheet to the Greek Life Office. The Greek Life Office enters your selections into its computer system. Once all the Potential New Members have submitted their selections, the Greek Life Office runs a report for each Potential New Member designating the sorority, the date, and time period for each third round of parties.

The third round of parties are exactly like the first two sets of parties, except that you spend an even longer length of time getting to know the sorority members. You may be asked to eat a dinner or a dessert with its active members. You should refer to, and be familiar with, the proper dining etiquette section of this Sorority Handbook prior to attending sorority parties in which meals are served. [See "Lesson 18: Table Etiquette" in this Handbook].

Again, if you attend a college campus that handles sorority Recruitment by invitation only, you are hand delivered an invitation to the third set by the specific sororities that invited you back.

If you have not yet received a house tour, each sorority takes you on a tour of the sorority house while its members attempt to get to know you on a more personal basis.

Additionally, you may have additional singing and speeches made by sorority members to communicate what sorority life and sisterhood means to them. You may be surprised that the "tone" in the sorority house is more serious than the previous visits which were more festive.

You make the final decision on which sororities you prefer to join after this party. The good news is that if you are invited back to the third round of parties, the sorority is considering you as a potential future member.

Pay extra close attention to the way you are interacting and feeling at this Third Visit. Do you like the other sorority members? Do you like the other Potential New Members who have been invited back? (They could be members of your pledge class). Do you share similar qualities with the sorority members? Are you being yourself? Are you feeling relaxed and comfortable? If not, why? A sorority house should feel like a second home to you. It should be a place that you find welcoming, supportive, and comfortable. Your intuition based on your feelings at each of the Recruitment parties should assist in guiding you to make decisions between sorority houses.

Potential New Members experience great disappointment if they do not receive an invitation to join in what they perceive as the "perfect" sorority. Keep in mind there is not necessarily one perfect choice. Consider all of your options (including a house that you may not have strongly considered earlier).

Joining a sorority is more than wearing Greek letters. You will devote time and energy to a sorority over your college career. Therefore, you need to keep an open mind and make an informed decision on what sorority is the best fit for you.

After the third round of parties, the active sorority members vote and rank all Potential New Members who have attended the third set of parties. The sororities poll the active members to either raise placards, hands, or submit a private voting sheet.

The Third Visit of voting is determinative on whether you are invited to be a member of its sorority. If you receive any "negative" cards or votes, the sorority may require that all active members who met you share a positive and negative attribute of having you as a member of their sorority. After discussing the positive and negative attributes, the sorority asks for a second vote. This second vote is your "score" and determines your final ranking.

The sorority submits its final list of Potential New Members to the Greek Life Office. The final list ranks Potential New Members into "positions/slots" of first choice, second choice, third choice, fourth choice etc. The Greek Life Office enters this information into its computer system.

The Third Visit is often referred to as the preference party visit because this is your *last* visit to the sorority house before you make your decision to rank the sororities from your favorite sorority (i.e. the one you are most interested in joining) to your least favorite sorority.

Unfortunately, when you submit your listing of your favorite to least favorite sororities, you do not know where you rank on the sorority's list (unless, the sorority violates Recruitment rules and discloses this information to you).

Basically, only two people know your final ranking in a sorority—the Recruitment Chairperson who submitted the list to the Greek Life Office and the Greek Life Office member assigned to input the sorority's Recruitment rankings into the computer.

Once you submit your ranking list, you cannot change your preference order. Let me remind you that this is your preference order, not your roommates', not your mother's, and not your best friend's.

Many Potential New Members complete preference cards based on their best friend's ranking. This is risky. You will be disappointed if you get your ranking's first choice (if in your heart it was your second choice) and your best friend gets her ranking's second choice (which was really your first choice). In short, neither one of you will be happy.

You now are asked to join a house that really was not your favorite. You conceivably filled the slot your best friend may have been able to take. Not only are you both unhappy with the outcome, but you also find yourselves in different sororities after all!

Think about it—if you rank a sorority based on the assumption that your best friend and you will be joining the sorority together, think again. When completing your preference card, make the decision based on what is best for you!

6.   *"Bid Day"/"New Member Day"*

You have made it to the end of Recruitment! Yippee, it is bid day (also may be called New Member Day)! This day should really be called match day because if your first choice listed you as its top choice you have a match.

Bid day is when you receive a bid to join a sorority. If your bid is matched, you will be notified with instructions on where to go; what to wear; and when you meet your new pledge sisters and sorority sisters. Often, special events or parties are planned to kick-off your pledge term!

Bid Day is often a day or evening of fun activities that include entertainment, pictures, and getting acquainted with new pledge sisters and sorority sisters. It marks the beginning of your "New Member Period" (or may be referred to as your "Pledgeship"). A New Member Period is the time the sorority dedicates to educating "New Members"/"Pledges" about the sorority's history and organizational structure.

During New Member Period, the sorority introduces you to all of its active members in the hopes that you will have an expanded circle of friends. The sorority is your new home away from home. The sorority may require you to eat a certain number of meals at the sorority; attend a certain amount of new member meetings; and attend sorority education meetings (e.g. learn about the history, philosophy and organizational structure of the sorority).

Last, many activities are held to build relations between the new members and the sorority sisters. Each new member may be given a "pledge mom" or "sorority mentor" who will take a special interest in getting to know you and introduce you to others in the sorority.

Some sororities will assign you a "big sister" during the "pledgeship" and other sororities will wait until after you have gone through the initiation ceremony. Big sisters are available to offer help and provide a positive experience with the sorority.

If you receive an invitation to join a sorority, you may be upset that your friends do not get invited to join any sorority. Or, you may be upset that you do not know anyone that received an invitation to your sorority. The good news is that you spend a lot of time with your pledge class and you will soon get to meet a lot of other pledges. Further, your friends who do not get invited to join a sorority will have the opportunity to meet people through you, as you will through them!

7. *What Happened? I (or my Best Friend) did not Receive a Bid to Join a Sorority.*

If your first sorority choice did not list you in its top quota ranking, it is up in the air on whether you will receive an invitation to join a sorority.

The bid is a lottery match process in that the computer will run everyone's first choices and all the matches will be paired together. For anyone that did not make a match, the computer re-runs the second choices to see if there is a match. Unfortunately, you can have "bad luck" in that had you ranked your second favorite sorority as your first choice you could have matched, but because you ranked the sorority as your second choice it now depends on how all of the other Potential New Members have matched whether you can obtain your second choice, third choice etc.

Bid Day is a very emotional day. Many people are devastated and cry on bid day thinking that not getting a bid from a sorority is a reflection on them and that their college days are doomed. Neither of these statements is true! [*See* "Lesson 10: Behind the Scenes" in this Handbook to learn how little control each Potential New Member has in the ultimate outcome of Recruitment].

Joining a sorority may seem like the most important event when going through the process, but there is much more to the college experience than being affiliated with a specific sorority. If you are determined to join a sorority, research whether you can go through Recruitment again mid-term, through Informal Recruitment or next year.

8. *Dropping Out of Recruitment or Declining an Invitation*

Recruitment is an opportunity for you to visit sororities and get a glimpse of sorority life. You always have the option of dropping out of the Recruitment process or declining to accept a sorority's invitation to join a house.

Sorority life does not appeal to everyone. Specifically, you may decide that joining a sorority is not for you, the time commitments during the New Member Period are too demanding, or the financial commitments of a particular sorority are too much.

Think carefully before making a decision to drop out of Recruitment or declining an invitation to join a sorority. Allow any emotions or heartbreak to subside before making this decision. Sometimes, if you give yourself or a sorority a chance, things will appear much better to you.

Whatever your reason for dropping out of Recruitment or declining an invitation to join a sorority, you may be prohibited from re-entering a future Recruitment period (including Continuous Open Bidding) if your college Greek Life Office rules so state.

LESSON 9

INFORMAL RECRUITMENT / RUSH

Colleges and Universities typically hold one Formal Recruitment period per year. This usually occurs in the fall. When the Formal Recruitment period officially ends on bid day, each sorority determines whether it has met its maximum quota that it submitted to the college's Greek Life Office prior to the Formal Recruitment process. If a sorority has not met its quota, it places a request at the college's Greek Life Office to enter into an Informal Recruitment period (also referred to as "Continuous Open Bidding").

If a sorority has not met its quota and enters into an Informal Recruitment period, it holds Informal Recruitment events. Many times these events take place during the spring or between terms/semesters. These events are sometimes referred to as Continuous Open Bidding events because it allows sororities an opportunity to take additional new members immediately following Formal Recruitment. It is a great opportunity for those women who have been "mismatched" (i.e. a Potential New Member does not match any of her sorority preferences) to join a sorority.

The sororities that enter into an Informal Recruitment period may advertise in local college papers, may contact you personally, or may rely on word of mouth. If you are interested in entering Informal Recruitment, you may be required to re-apply to your college's Greek Life Office. The Greek Life Office forwards this information to each individual sorority chapter that has elected to enter into an Informal Recruitment period. Again, these rules may vary from campus to campus. Therefore, refer to your college's Recruitment guide in determining the correct procedure for your college campus.

Not as many bids/invitations to join sororities are offered during Informal Recruitment. Informal Recruitment has no schedules. The responsibility for Informal Recruitment is between the sorority and the Potential New Members still eligible to join a sorority. Informal Recruitment allows sorority houses and Potential New Members to plan meetings and activities on their own schedules. During the Informal Recruitment process, a sorority can invite a Potential New Member to join its sorority at any time allowed by the college's Greek Life Office. If a Potential New Member accepts a bid during Informal Recruitment, the Potential New Member is placed in the current pledge class year with the other members in the pledge class who were accepted during the Formal Recruitment period.

Lesson 10

Behind the Scenes

1. *The Sorority Prepares for Recruitment*

If you think you are nervous about the Recruitment process, just ask any Recruitment Chairperson and she will tell you that the Recruitment process is nerve-wracking and important to the sorority too.

The sorority is charged with making its quota, presenting a positive house, and keeping its current active sorority members involved in the selection process.

Besides having the sorority cleaned and organized before Recruitment, a lot of planning goes into the sorority Recruitment process.

The Recruitment Chairperson and Assistant Recruitment Chairperson must develop a schedule for the entire sorority that indicates what is expected of each sorority member.

Specifically, if any active sorority member is going to be a Recruitment Counselor, Greek Life Office volunteer, or is not participating in the Recruitment process, all photographs and names containing their identities must be removed from a Potential New Member's view.

Further, all Recruitment information sheets and reference letters must be assembled and posted in an area of the sorority house that each member of the house can easily view, but that the Potential New Members cannot see during the Recruitment process.

All Recruitment information sheets and reference letters must be acknowledged [*See* "Lesson 11: Reference Letter and Legacies" in this Handbook for an in-depth discussion].

All legacy information must be posted. (Note: many sororities automatically invite legacies to the second or third party without voting on the Potential New Member.)

All Potential New Members' names, pictures, information sheets, reference letters and legacy information are read to the active sorority members before each party. Active sorority members are encouraged to seek these individuals out.

All skits, videos, songs, and dances are rehearsed before the Recruitment process and performed throughout the Recruitment process.

Each sorority member must be given an adequate number of "scorecards". The scorecards are hidden from the Potential New Members during the Recruitment process. The scorecards are often hidden under furniture or cushions so the scorecards are readily available to document information as soon as the Potential New Members leave the sorority house.

Active sorority members may not communicate with any Potential New Members during the designated "quiet periods". "Quiet periods" are when sororities hold meetings to make decisions about Potential New Members. Potential New Members may not have any contact or communication with sorority actives, alumni, house mothers or anyone else associated with sorority Recruitment.

Active sorority members must not divulge any portion of the sorority process to other Potential New Members.

2. *The Sorority during Recruitment*

Active sorority members must record the name of every Potential New Member they meet and indicate any information that will "jog" their memory about the Potential New Member for formal voting (e.g. where are they from, any defining or unusual characteristics that will remind the active sorority member about the Potential New Member during voting).

Unfortunately, not all active sorority members are alike. As a Potential New Member, you have an equal chance of meeting a friendly/outgoing active member or a reserved/shy active member of a sorority. The friendly member is going to take you around and introduce you to as many people as possible. This is good for you because you have the opportunity for more votes and more people "campaigning" for you. On the other hand, if you get a more reserved/shy member, she may not introduce you to as many people, she may not "campaign" for you, and she may remain quiet during the voting process.

Unfortunately, you have no control over who is assigned to you when you go through the sorority door. You are paired with an active sorority member based on where you fall in line when entering the sorority.

If you are disappointed that you did not get invited back to the house, it may be because the quiet, shy, and reserved active did not like public speaking and sat "quietly" through the voting process.

On the other hand, if you have an active sorority member that was loud and boisterous, but the sorority sisters dislike her, you may not be invited back simply because they did not like the person campaigning for you. Again, it is not a reflection on you and has nothing to do with what you may have or have not done.

Remember, like all other organizations, sorority sisters do not necessarily like everyone else in the sorority. Just like high school, there are cliques and sub-cliques inside a sorority house.

Ask anyone that has ever been in a sorority, and she may tell you that she really liked some of the sorority members, others she tolerated and others she disliked (although she may have never stated so during college).

Imagine a sorority having 110 active members. Imagine 110 females at your high school. Can you really conceive of having 110 female best friends?

Now imagine it is sorority Recruitment, assume that there are 11 cliques in a sorority house and each of the cliques has 10 friends. Each of the cliques' campaign for prospective candidates. Can you imagine voting time? Hands down, the Potential New Members that make it to the top of the quota ranking list are those Potential New Members supported by multiple "cliques".

Again, if you are not selected into a sorority, do not blame yourself—you can blame it on whomever you were matched with at the sorority or bad luck. I know you may be disappointed, but it is not an indication of you, your personality, or your approachability.

Every year, active sorority sisters are "shocked" to find out that some "top" women, being recruited hard by many sororities, do not receive an invitation to bid any sorority. Unfortunately, the matching/selection process is not perfect.

The worst mistake any Potential New Member can make is to tell a favorite sorority they are a legacy of another sorority. It is automatically assumed that you want to join the sorority where you are a legacy, when in fact you may like other sororities better.

By divulging legacy information from another house, you may hurt your chances to join a sorority in which you are not a legacy. On the other hand, if you are visiting a sorority where you are a legacy and you like the sorority, by all means, tell them that your family member was not only a member of that particular sorority, but also has many fond memories of the sorority.

LESSON 11

REFERENCE LETTERS & LEGACIES

1. *Reference Letters/Recommendation Letters*

Reference letters (also referred to as recommendation letters, letters of introduction or information sheets) are letters or statements from an alumna (a female graduate) recommending a woman for membership. An alumna can only write a recommendation for her own sorority.

Reference letters provide a more personal introduction to you and assist sororities in obtaining information on you prior to the Recruitment period.

Each national sorority has its own standard form for providing reference letters. If a form is not available, or the deadline for submitting reference letters is quickly approaching, a personal letter may be written instead. Generally, sororities must receive reference letters by late-July to mid-August.

A reference letter often contains information on the number of years the alumna has known you, what type of relationship that the alumna has with you; what high school activities you are involved in; your grade point average; and a brief statement about why you would be a valued member of this sorority. Specifically, what skills, talents, and characteristics do you possess that can contribute to the sorority. Often times, a picture of you will be sent with the reference letter.

Reference letters are not required in all sororities. Reference letters vary in importance for different sororities on different campuses. Reference letters are critical on college campuses with well-established and highly competitive sororities.

Reference letters are not a guarantee that you will receive an invitation or a bid from any sorority. Nevertheless, reference letters allow you the opportunity to be automatically invited back to the second round of events/parties for some sororities on some college campuses. You will not be privy to knowing what sororities on what campuses follow this automatic invitation process. Thus, I encourage you to ask your family members, neighbors, and family friends if they are alumnae of any sorority. If so, ask them to write a reference letters on your behalf to their sororities. (BEWARE: Do not ask alumnae to write reference letters for you unless you are certain that it will be a positive letter.)

Give the alumna writing the reference letter a copy of your "resume". The alumna can either contact her sorority to request a standard form or send a personal letter and attach a copy of your resume and photograph. It is the alumna's responsibility to complete and return the reference letter by the imposed deadline.

Please do not expect that the alumna writing you a reference letter to provide you with a copy. Under no circumstances should you personally contact sororities to obtain copies of references submitted on your behalf. Further, do not contact sororities to verify whether any reference letters were received on your behalf. In short, the alumna providing the reference letter initiates contact with the sorority.

2.   *Legacies*

Generally, a legacy is defined as a daughter, granddaughter, great granddaughter or sister of an initiated sorority member. Sometimes a legacy can include aunts, cousins, or relatives by marriage. If any of your family members are alumna of a sorority, you are considered a legacy of that sorority. Further, you may be a legacy to more than one sorority.

A legacy is not obligated to join a particular sorority. Likewise, a sorority is not required to pledge all of its legacies. Sororities usually give legacies some extra consideration by receiving an automatic invitation back to the second round of events/parties. Potential New Members and sororities are looking for a compatible fit more than a family connection to the national organization.

Sororities have various policies on legacies, but most sororities will invite legacies back to an additional event as a courtesy, which allows additional time for you and the sorority to get to know each other. Thus, being a legacy of a particular sorority may assist you in being invited back to an additional sorority event that you may not otherwise have been invited back to visit.

3. *No Reference, No Legacy . . . . No Problem*

If you do not know anyone who will write a reference for you or you are not a legacy of any sorority chapter, it is not detrimental to the Recruitment process. You can still become a member of a sorority.

Many Potential New Members believe that if someone has references on file with a sorority or has legacy status, that those Potential New Members somehow have an advantage. While references and legacy information does assist a sorority in getting to know Potential New Members prior to Formal Recruitment, it is not a major advantage. Keep in mind that a sorority is not obligated to pledge its legacies. Further, the entire point of going through Recruitment is so all Potential New Members have an equal chance of joining a sorority.

Ultimately, sororities offer bids to Potential New Members based on friendship, not on reference letters/recommendations or legacy status.

Lesson 12

"It's All Greek to Me"
Sorority Vocabulary

Active	A member of the sorority who is in good standing. She has gone through the pledge process and has been initiated.
Alpha Delta Kappa National Educators Honorary Sorority	An international honorary sorority for women educators.
Alumna	An initiated sorority member who is no longer enrolled in college.
Alumnae	Plural of alumna; initiated sorority members who are no longer enrolled in college.
Alumnae Panhellenic	The local chapter/organization of the alumnae of the National Panhellenic Conference sororities in your city or geographical area.
Badge/Pin (two different types)	An active pin/badge is worn on the chest. It is ornate and is given at initiation. A new member pin is simple looking in appearance and is given on pledge day.
Basileus	The highest leaders of the sorority organization. [i.e. Supreme Basileus (President); Grand Basileus (Vice President)].
Bid	An official invitation to join a sorority.
Bid Day	The last day of sorority Recruitment in which you receive a bid to join a particular sorority and you will often have activities planned to welcome you to the sorority.
Big Sister	An active member of the sorority who is assigned to mentor you and communicate sorority information to you once you have become initiated.
Chapter	The name applied to the local group of a national sorority and designated by a special Greek alphabet letter(s). For example, Chi Omega is a national sorority. Chi Omega is on many college campuses. In order for the national sorority to refer to specific locations, it will state Chi Omega and include a (Greek alphabet letter) following it. For example, Chi Omega, Eta Chapter designates the Chi Omega house at the University of Michigan.
College Fraternity Editors Association (CFEA)	CFEA promotes high standards in sorority and fraternity journalism and communications. Membership is comprised of Greek letter sororities, fraternities, professional and honorary groups.

College Panhellenic Office	A cooperative college organization of its sororities. The College Panhellenic Office is where a prospective member ("Potential New Member" or "Rushee") must register in order to join Formal Recruitment.
Continuous Open Bidding	If a sorority has not met its quota, it will place a request at the college Greek Life Office to enter into an Informal Recruitment period, which allows sororities to offer invitations to bid sororities after the Formal Recruitment
Cut	A prospective sorority member is not invited back to join the sorority.
Deferred Recruitment / Deferred Rush	A"Recruitment" or "Rush" week scheduled at a time other than the opening of school.
Depledge / Depledging	A pledge decides to drop out of the sorority after accepting an invitation to join a sorority, but before initiation.
Dry Recruitment / Dry Rush	No alcohol is allowed at sorority functions
Early Bid / Early Invitation	A sorority member receives a bid from a sorority before the official bid day. Many Formal Recruitment periods do not allow for early bids/early invitations.
FIPG	FIPG manages collegiate risk management programs by promoting policies and practices in Greek Life.
Formal Parties / Functions	The social gatherings scheduled at a specific time in association with Formal Recruitment.
Formal Recruitment /Formal Rush	The Formal Recruitment/Rush period designated by your university. It is usually a series of events hosted by sororities during a given period scheduled by and governed by college Greek Life offices.
Formal Recruitment Acceptance Card	An invitation to join a sorority.
Fraternity	The name designated to all Greek letter organizations (fraternities and sororities). Informally, the name is referred to designate the groups/houses for college men.
Fraternity Executives Association	Organization composed of administrative officers from the NIC and NPC. It promotes, supports, and encourages discussions and ideas relating to college fraternal organizations.
Free Sis / Sitting Sis	A Potential New Member that is going through the Recruitment process and has a sister who is an active member
Gamma Sigma Alpha National Greek Honor	Promotes intellectual interaction between Greek students and academics to encourage excellence in scholarship.
Gifts	A Potential New Member must not give or receive any gifts during the Recruitment process. If a Potential New Member receives a gift during an event at a sorority house, she must leave it at the sorority.
Golden Key National Honor Society	Nonprofit academic organization that provides economic assistance by providing undergraduate and graduate scholarships to its outstanding members.
Greek	A member of a fraternity or a sorority.
Guaranteed Placement	At some colleges, a Potential New Member is guaranteed to get accepted into a sorority as long as she has attended all of the parties to which she has been invited.
Hazing	Hazing is illegal in most states. Hazing is defined as doing things that are against your will, violate you, or could cause you imminent harm.

Hold Over / Continuous New Member	A new member who does not meet the scholastic standards necessary to join a sorority. The new member is not allowed to become initiated until the scholastic requirements are achieved.
Hot Boxing	Any situation where a potential member is intentionally separated or isolated from typical Recruitment activities by conversation or position. Usually this involves an unequal ratio of actives to Potential New Members or heavily pressuring Potential New Members to accept a sorority's invitation to join.
House Mother / House Director	A woman who lives with the sorority's active members and manages the sorority house. The House Mother/House Director plans meal, coordinates house repairs, collects sorority rent/dues, enforces house safety, and maintains the sorority. This is a paid position. Current college students are not eligible to hold this position.
Informal Parties / Functions	Parties that do not follow specific university or national organization schedules.
Informal Recruitment	An unorganized Recruitment; the Potential New Member can meet sorority members at anytime. The recruitment period occurs at various times throughout the year.
Initiate	A woman who has recently become an active member of her sorority after the New Member Period has been completed.
Initiation	A formal ceremony in which a pledge/new member becomes an active (full membership into the sorority). Active members will reveal secret handshakes, secret ceremonies, secret code words and provide you with sorority's history and/or rituals.
Intentional Single Preference	At the end of Recruitment week, a Potential New Member chooses only one sorority despite attending two or more preferential parties. If a Potential New Member only chooses one preference to join a sorority, the chances of joining any sorority are decreased.
Interfraternity Council (IFC)	The governing body of the North American Interfraternity Conference for men fraternities.
Lavaliere	A Greek letter necklace; Sorority members often receive their Lavalieres at the pledge sorority or invitation sorority.
Legacy	A woman whose mother and/or sister, (or in some cases grandmother and great grandmother), is an initiated sorority member. Legacy definitions differ for each sorority. It is possible to be a legacy to more than one sorority. A sorority is not obligated to offer bids to its legacies.
Membership Intake	The term used to meet the Recruitment requirements of the National Pan—Hellenic Council (NPHC) sororities.
Mismatch	A Potential New Member does not match any of her sorority preferences.
National Association of Latino Fraternal Organizations (NALFO)	A national organization of predominantly Latino Sororities in the Greek Community as members.
National Interfraternity Conference (NIC)	A national organization composed of 67 member men's fraternities in the United States and Canada. Each member organization is a Greek letter society consisting of college men and alumni.

National Panhellenic Conference (NPC)	A national governing organization composed of 26 member women's fraternities, that makes rules and regulations for the sororities in the Panhellenic conference. Each member group is autonomous as a social, Greek letter society of college women and alumnae
National Pan-Hellenic Conference (NPHC)	A national governing organization that makes rules and regulations for nine historically African-American fraternities and sororities. Racism prevented many African-American students on historically white campuses from joining general fraternities and sor
New Member / Pledge	A woman who has accepted the bid offered by a sorority and has taken the first step toward full membership, but has not yet been initiated into the sorority.
New Member Class/ Pledge Class	The group of New Members / Pledges that join a sorority at the same time.
New Member Educator	Sorority officer who coordinates the education for the sorority's new members.
New Member Meetings / Pledge Meetings	Special meetings held during the Pledgeship for new members to learn the history of the sorority as well as to learn about important issues affecting college women regarding safety and study skills.
New Member Mom / Pledge Mom	An active member of the sorority that is assigned to mentor a pledge and communicate sorority information to a pledge.
New Member Period / Pledgeship	A period of time dedicated to educating a pledge about a sorority chapter's history and organizational structure. A Pledgeship/New Member Period is similar to an orientation and some new member classes elect officers, hold meetings, organize social events
Omicron Delta Kappa National Leadership Honor Society	National leadership honor society for college students, faculty, staff, and alumni to recognize leadership, scholarship and exemplary character.
Open Recruitment	The period following Formal Recruitment/Rush when there may be Informal Recruitment with no scheduled parties.
Oral Bidding	A statement by a sorority member which leads you to believe that you are invited to join a sorority. For example, "I want you to live here"; "you would make a great little sister for me"; or "you belong in this sorority" falsely imply an invitation to join a sorority. No individual member has the authority to issue invitations or guarantee membership.
Order of Omega Honor Society	Encourages fraternity men and sorority women to attain a high standard of leadership in interfraternity activities.
Panhellenic	A word meaning "all Greek".
Panhellenic Council	It is the governing body of all National Panhellenic Conference sororities. The Panhellenic Council facilitates relationships between sororities, the college, and the community by coordinating events and developing policies.

Philanthropy	A sorority chooses a designated charity to raise money or awareness for an organization. Philanthropy is defined as "service to others" and is an important part of a sorority's creed.
Pin	A sorority member's badge of membership.
Pinned	A fraternity boy gives his fraternity pin to express his love and affection to a sorority girl. It can also be considered to be construed as a "promise ring" that the couple has a future together.
Pledge / New Member	A Potential New Member who has accepted a sorority's bid, but has not yet been initiated.
Pledgeship / New Member Period	A period of time dedicated to educating a pledge about a sorority chapter's history and organizational structure. A Pledgeship/New Member Period is similar to an orientation and some new member classes elect officers, hold meetings, organize social events, and plan study programs.
Pledge Class / New Member Class	The group of Pledges/New Members that join a sorority at the same time.
Pledge Leader / Pledge Educator	Active sorority member(s) who act as a liaison between the pledge class and the sorority chapter house. Pledge leaders plan the pledge program.
Pledge Meetings / New Member Meetings	Special meetings held during the New Member Period / Pledgeship for new members to learn the history of the sorority as well as to learn about important issues affecting college women regarding safety and study skills.
Pledge Mom / New Member Mom	An active member of the sorority that is assigned to mentor a pledge and communicate sorority information to a pledge.
Pledge Pin / New Member Pin	A pin/badge given to a new member in recognition of pledging/initiating into a sorority.
Potential New Member / Rushee	A college woman who is participating in the Recruitment/Rush process.
Preference Cards	The official cards Potential New Members complete when choosing which sorority parties that they would like to attend.
Preference Parties	The final parties that a Potential New Member attends before the formal bid process begins.
Preferential Bidding	The formal system used to conclude the formal Recruitment/Rush when sororities and Potential New Members indicate their sorority choices.
Quiet Time / Quiet Hours / Silence	A designated time period when sororities hold meetings to make decisions about Potential New Members. The time period is designated by the Greek Life Office and it usually occurs during Formal Recruitment/Rush. Potential New Members may not have any contact/communication with actives, alumni, house mothers, or anyone else associated with the sorority.
Quota	The maximum number of new members that a sorority can select during a Recruitment period. Each sorority is entitled to take a quota of new members and cannot exceed the quota determined by the Greek Life Office prior to Formal Recruitment/Rush.
Recommendation / Reference Letter	A form used by a sorority to obtain information about a Potential New Member.

Reference Letter / Recommendation	A letter in support of a woman for membership. It is written by an alumna sorority member to her sorority organization. Note: If the woman writing your reference graduated from a different college/university than the one that you are attending, she can still provide you with a reference letter.
Resume	A Potential New Member's information sheet.
Rho Chi / Recruitment Counselor / RC	Rho Chi is the Greek initials for RC, which stands for Recruitment Counselor/Rush Counselor. She is a sorority member who is trained by the Greek Life Office to be a guide during Recruitment. She is available to assist you and clarify "rumors" attributable to sororities.
Rho Lambda	Rho Lambda honors Panhellenic women who have exhibited the highest qualities of leadership and service to their sorority and Panhellenic.
Ritual	A traditional ceremony for each sorority. It differs by national sorority. For example, the Thetas and Kappas have different rituals.
Recruitment / Rush	The time period designated by the Greek Life Office in which sororities choose new members through a mutual selection process.
Rushee / Potential New Member /Collegian	A prospective sorority member.
Recruitment Counselor / Rho Chi / RC	An active sorority member who has given up her sorority association during Recruitment. Potential New Members are typically divided into Recruitment groups by the last name. A Recruitment Counselor is assigned to ensure that the Potential New Members attend each event on time, the Recruitment rules are obeyed, and that the Recruitment runs well.
Recruitment Group	Potential New Members are typically divided in groups by the last name. The Potential New Member will stay with the Recruitment group while the Potential New Members are attending sorority events during the Formal Recruitment process.
Silence	A designated period of time when contact between the potential new members and sorority actives are strictly limited by the Panhellenic Recruitment Rules. This silence period also extends to its alumnae and agents of the sororities.
Sitting Sis / Free Sis	A Potential New Member who is going through the Recruitment process and has a sister who is an active member in a sorority.
Sorority	A women's fraternity also called a Greek Letter Sisterhood. Sorority means sisterhood in Latin.

Lesson 13

Sororities Galore

All sororities encourage sisterhood, scholarship, socializing, leadership, and service to others. If you are interested in learning about sororities on a national level, take time to visit their national Internet website. If you are interested in learning about sororities on a local level, contact your college's Greek Life Office and ask for the Internet address specific to your college's sorority chapter.

1. *African American Sororities*

    African American Sororities are part of the National Pan-Hellenic Council, Inc. (NPHC). The NPHC, established in 1930 at Howard University, is the national governing body for five historically African-American Fraternities and four historically African-American Sororities. Racism prevented many African-American students on historically white campuses from joining "traditional" fraternities and sororities. Thus, African-American students established fraternities and sororities to enhance their college experiences. These organizations do not restrict membership to African-Americans.

    You must contact your college campus' Pan-Hellenic Council Office or Greek Life Office to obtain Recruitment information.

The Sororities governed by the National Pan-Hellenic Council are as follows:

Sorority Name	Greek Letters	Internet Address
Alpha Kappa Alpha	AKA	www.aka1908.com
Delta Sigma Theta	ΔΣΘ	www.deltasigmatheta.net
Zeta Phi Beta	ZΦB	www.zphib1920.org
Sigma Gamma Rho	ΣΓΡ	www.sgrho1922.org

To find out more about these sororities on a national level, visit their Internet websites or contact the NPHC office by visiting its Internet site at www.nphchq.org or writing to:

NPHC Headquarters
Memorial Hall West 111
Bloomington, Indiana 47405

812/855-8820 (Telephone)
812/856-5477 (Facsimile)

2. *Asian-American Sororities*

The oldest Asian sorority was chartered in 1928 at UCLA, but became inactive when the majority of its members were unable to attend college during World War II.

Since World War II, Asian—American Sororities provide a common bond for Asians to become a part of a sisterhood with those that have similar cultural backgrounds.

New Asian-American sororities continue to form on college campuses. Thus, it is imperative to contact your college campus' Greek Life Office to obtain Recruitment information on the

Asian-American sororities that have formed on your college campus, as this list is subject to change at any given time.

Sorority Name	Greek Letters	Internet Address
alpha Kappa Delta Phi	ΑκδΘ	www.akdphi.org
Sigma Omicron Pi	ΣΟΠ	www.sigmaomicronpi.com
Kappa Phi Lambda	ΚΦΛ	www.kappaphilambda.org
Alpha Phi Gamma	ΑΦΓ	www.alphaphigamma.org
Delta Phi Omega (South Asian Sorority)	ΔΦΩ	www.deltaphiomega.org
Kappa Phi Gamma (South Asian Sorority)	ΚΦΓ	www.kappaphigamma.org
Chi Sigma Phi	ΧΣΦ	www.chisigmaphi.com
Sigma Psi Zeta	ΣΨΖ	www.sigmapsizeta.org

3. **Christian Sororities**

Christian Sororities provide the same benefits of "sisterhood" as Greek letter sororities while incorporating religious study into its chapters. For a current listing of Christian sororities on your college campus, contact your college's Greek Life Office or Student Life Office or for a listing of campuses that have Christian sororities visit the following Internet site: www.groups.msn.com/ChristianFraternitiesandSororities/chapters.msnw.

4. **Latina Sororities**

Many, but not all, Latina Sororities are members of the

National Association of Latino Fraternal Organizations (NALFO). Established in 1998, NALFO is the umbrella council for Latino Greek Letter Organizations for fraternities and sororities. NALFO promotes and fosters communication and development of Latino organizations through its stated principals of mutual respect, leadership, honesty, professionalism and education.

To find out more about these NALFO sororities on a national level, visit their Internet websites or contact NALFO by visiting its Internet site at www.nalfo.org.

To learn about other Latina sororities (that are not members of NALFO or new on your college campus), contact your college campus' Greek Life Office. Your college's Greek Life Office has Recruitment information on the Latina sororities on your college campus, as this list contains only those sororities that are part of NALFO. Further, this list is subject to change at any given time.

Sorority Name	Greek Letters	Internet Address
Alpha Pi Sigma	ΑΠΣ	www.alphapisigma.org
Alpha Rho Lambda	ΑΡΛ	www.alpharholambda.org
Gamma Phi Omega	ΓΦΩ	www.gammaphiomega.org
Kappa Delta Chi	ΚΔΧ	www.kappadeltachi.org
Lambda Theta Alpha	ΛΘΑ	www.latinogreeks.com
Lambda Theta Nu	ΛΘΝ	www.lambdathetanu.org
Lambda Pi Upsilon	ΛΠΥ	www.lpiu.com

Lambda Pi Chi	ΛΠΧ	www.lambdapichi.com
Hermandad de Sigma Iota Alpha	Hermandad de ΣΙΑ	www.hermandad-SIA.org
Sigma Lambda Gamma	ΣΛΓ	www.sigmalambdagamma.com
Sigma Lambda Upsilon	ΣΛΥ	www.sigmalambdaupsilon.org
Chi Upsilon Sigma	ΧΥΣ	www.justbeCUS.org
Omega Phi Beta	ΩΦΒ	www.omegaphibeta.org

5. *Jewish Sororities*

Jewish sororities were founded in the early decades of the last century, when Jews were excluded from "Greek" life on college campuses. Jewish sororities promote unity, support, and awareness to its members and communities.

To find out more Jewish sororities on a national level, visit their Internet websites.

Sorority Name	Greek Letters	Internet Address
Alpha Epsilon Phi (Nickname "A E	ΑΕΦ	www.aephi.org
Delta Phi Epsilon (Nickname "D Phi	ΔΦΕ	www.dphie.org
Sigma Delta Tau (Nicknames "SDT" or "Sig Delts")	ΣΔΤ	www.sigmadeltatau.com

6.   *Military Sororities*

Sigma Phi Psi is the first Greek Letter Sorority established by and for the U. S. Armed Forces Women (Army, Navy, Marines, Air Force, and Coast Guard). The women come from diverse cultures and are unified by one common goal of "success against all odds."

To learn more about this Military Sorority, visit its Internet site.

Sorority Name	Greek Letters	Internet Address
Sigma Phi Psi	ΣΦΨ	www.sigmaphipsi.org

7. Native American Sororities

Alpha Pi Omega Sorority, Inc., is the first Native American Sorority in the nation. Alpha Pi Omega was founded at the University of North Carolina (Chapel Hill) on September 1, 1994. Alpha Pi Omega's principles are founded on traditionalism, spirituality, education, and contemporary issues. Its focus is to increase awareness of Native American culture and issues.

Sorority Name	Greek Letters	Internet Address
Alpha Pi Omega	ΑΠΩ	www.unc.edu/student/orgs/apiomega/

8. Panhellenic Sororities

In the past, the sororities portrayed most often by Hollywood in movies and television are Panhellenic sororities. Panhellenic is a Greek word meaning "all Greek".

There are 26 member sororities in the National Panhellenic Conference ("NPC"). Panhellenic sororities are social, Greek letter organizations of college women and alumnae. The NPC is the national governing association for providing rules and regulations at a local level.

To find out more about these sororities on a national level, visit their Internet websites or contact the NPC office by visiting its Internet site at www.npcwomen.org or writing to:

NPC
3905 Vincennes Road, Suite 105
Indianapolis, Indiana 46268

317/872-3185 (Telephone)
317/872-3192 (Facsimile)

The Sororities governed by the National Panhellenic Conference are as follows:

Sorority Name	Greek Letters	Internet Address
Pi Beta Phi (Nickname "Pi Phi")	ΠΒΦ	www.pibetaphi.org
Kappa Alpha Theta (Nickname "Theta")	ΚΑΘ	www.kappaalphatheta.org
Kappa Kappa Gamma (Nickname "Kappa")	ΚΚΓ	www.kappakappagamma.org
Alpha Phi (Nickname "Alpha Phi")	ΑΦ	www.alphaphi.org
Delta Gamma (Nickname "DG")	ΔΓ	www.deltagamma.org
Gamma Phi Beta (Nickname "Gamma Phi")	ΓΦΒ	www.gammaphibeta.org
Delta Delta Delta (Nickname "Tri—Delt")	ΔΔΔ	www.tridelta.org
Alpha Xi Delta (Nickname "AZD")	ΑΞΔ	www.alphaxidelta.org
Alpha Chi Omega (Nicknames "Alpha Chi" or "A Chi O")	ΑΧΩ	www.alphachiomega.org

Chi Omega (Often referred to as "Chi O")	ΧΩ	www.chiomega.com
Sigma Kappa (Nickname "Sigma K")	ΣΚ	www.sigmakappa.org
Alpha Omicron Pi (Nickname "A O Pi")	ΑΟΠ	www.alphaomicronpi.org
Zeta Tau Alpha (Nickname "Zeta")	ΖΤΑ	www.zetataualpha.org
Alpha Gamma Delta (Nicknames "Alpha Gam" or "AGD")	ΑΓΔ	www.alphagammadelta.org
Alpha Delta Pi (Nickname "A D Pi")	ΑΔΠ	www.alphadeltapi.org
Delta Zeta (Nickname "DZ")	ΔΖ	www.deltazeta.org
Phi Mu (Nickname "Phi Mu")	ΦΜ	www.phimu.org
Kappa Delta (Nickname "KD")	ΚΔ	www.kappadelta.org
Sigma Sigma Sigma (Nickname "Tri-Sigma")	ΣΣΣ	www.sigmasigmasigma.org
Alpha Sigma Tau (Nickname "AST")	ΑΣΤ	www.alphasigmatau.org
Alpha Sigma Alpha (Nickname "ASA")	ΑΣΑ	www.alphasigmaalpha.org
Alpha Epsilon Phi (Nickname "AEPhi")	ΑΕΦ	www.aephi.org
Theta Phi Alpha	ΘΦΑ	www.thetaphialpha.org
Phi Sigma Sigma (Nickname "Phi Sig")	ΦΣΣ	www.phisigmasigma.org
Delta Phi Epsilon (Nickname "D Phi E")	ΔΦΕ	www.dphie.org
Sigma Delta Tau (Nicknames "SDT" or "Sig Delts")	ΣΔΤ	www.sigmadeltatau.com

9. *Service Based Sororities (e.g. music, choir, band)*

Many colleges have service based sororities for those interested
in music, band, or choir. You must contact your college
Student Services Department or the Greek Life Office to
determine whether any service based sororities are on your
college campus. If so, ask for the national Internet website or
local Internet website to determine criteria for joining and
the list of Recruitment/Rush dates. Generally, service based
sororities are open to anyone who wishes to learn more about
music, band, or choir.

LESSON 14

JOINING A SORORITY CHECKLIST

Are you considering joining a sorority during your freshman year at college? Colleges recommend that you register for sorority Recruitment, even if you are not interested in joining a sorority. You can drop out of the sorority Recruitment process at any time, but you cannot register for it late. You will not know exactly how you feel about joining a sorority until you arrive at your college campus in the fall.

You need to get started on the following checklist in order to join a sorority:

————— As soon as you are accepted to a college, visit its Internet site and find the sororities at your college campus.

————— Ask your school guidance counselor if college sorority "Information Nights" are being held locally.

————— Create and maintain a file so you can access all sorority Recruitment information easily.

————— Sign up for the "Information Night" meeting and encourage your parents to attend.

————— Develop a "resume" of your accomplishments.

————— Attend "Information Night" and pick-up an "Information Form" at the meeting.

————— Prepare an information statement that lists high school/ college activities, awards, honors, and community activities. This will assist you when completing your

Recruitment packet. This will assist others if they are providing references/recommendations for you.

_____ Make copies of all Recruitment information that you submit to your college and local alumnae groups.

_____ Complete your Information Form and return before the stated deadline (usually in mid-June).

_____ Attach a "resume" of your accomplishments and an informal photograph of you to the Information Form.

_____ Obtain a copy of your high school grade transcripts so you can have this information should it be required.

_____ Re-visit your University's Internet site to obtain information about the Formal Recruitment process.

_____ Request Recruitment paperwork from your college's Greek Life Office.

_____ Ask if the Recruitment paperwork contains an instructions checklist. If so follow the checklist completely to expedite your Recruitment application.

_____ Read the paperwork that the college sent you. The information may contain extremely important Recruitment dates, deadlines, procedures, and financial obligations.

_____ Register for the Recruitment process.

_____ Write the Recruitment dates down on your calendar. Make plans to attend all Recruitment parties.

_____ Determine whether you will need to make alternative housing reservations (e.g. hotel reservations) if your Recruitment period begins before you are able to move into a dorm or other campus housing.

_____ Schedule your college summer orientation so it does not conflict with Recruitment parties or Parent/Daughter information nights.

_____ Pay Recruitment registration fees.

_____ Submit Recruitment paperwork before the deadline.

_____ Provide copies of your high school transcripts, if requested.

_____ Locate at least two people that are willing to be a

Recruitment reference for you (e.g. teachers, neighbors, employers). Note: this is not the same as providing a Formal Recruitment reference or recommendation from a member of a specific sorority. This is a general recommendation and is required for Recruitment at some college campuses.

_____ Ask friends, neighbors, mothers, sisters, and grandmothers who were members of college sororities to write "Letters of Reference" (formerly referred to as "Recommendations") on your behalf. Each chapter at each college has a designated due date in which to receive reference letters. Your reference must send the reference letters to the appropriate person(s) prior to any deadlines.

_____ Obtain the name of the sorority, college attended, and year your sister, mother, grandmother joined a sorority. You may need to provide this information in your Recruitment packet.

_____ Talk to your parents about the financial and academic requirements of sorority membership.

_____ Verify whether you can meet the financial obligations of joining a sorority—social dues, housing and food expenses (if you are required to live in the sorority).

_____ Make a hotel reservation if your college campus begins Recruitment *before* the official school year begins.

_____ Attend all group parties offered in the summer that are sponsored by the alumnae associations.

_____ Pay all required fees.

_____ Request a refund, if it is necessary to cancel your Recruitment registration.

LESSON 15

RECRUITMENT / RUSH TIPS

These Recruitment tips not only prepare you to join a sorority, but also are valuable tips to use in your everyday personal and professional life.

These are the same tips that to use while interviewing for a job, meeting people for the first time, or giving a presentation. In short, these tips will not only serve you well during the Recruitment process, but they will serve you well in life. Keep the following Recruitment tips in mind while visiting sorority houses:

- **Be yourself.**

  Recruitment by its very nature is not a true indicator of how a person acts on a daily basis. The active sorority members and the Potential New Members are both trying to make a good impression. The sorority is trying to "sell" the Potential New Member on the sorority. The Potential New Member is trying to join the sorority. It does not take a rocket scientist to guess that people are going to be overly nice, friendly, and outgoing during Recruitment. Yes, some sorority members and some Potential New Members may sound like they are "faking" their niceness. If you understand that everyone involved in the Recruitment process is trying to make a good impression, you will be more tolerant of those that seem to be faking their interest and friendliness. Be yourself, because when you are yourself, others will be more likely to let down their guards and be themselves too.

- **Keep an open mind.**

  As you prepare for Recruitment, enter into it with an open mind. Think of it as a new adventure in your life. Be an explorer—enter with curiosity and confidence. Even though you are not hosting the event, be friendly and inviting. Relax and, above all else, have fun!

- **Create a lasting first impression.**

  First impressions are lasting ones. You never get a second chance to make a first impression. Look at yourself in a full-length mirror. Do you like what you see? Is your hair clean and combed? Are your teeth brushed? Are your hands and face washed? If you wear make-up, does it look natural? Are your fingernails and toenails manicured and clean? Are your clothes neat, clean, and ironed/pressed? [The quality, style and brand name of clothes are not as important as the cleanliness and neatness of clothes.] Finally, discard the chewing gum and breath mints before you meet and greet!

- **Maintain a personal space.**

  Stand a comfortable distance away from the person with whom you are speaking. Stand within an arms length from an individual during introductions. If you stand too close, you communicate a "panicky over eagerness." Be clam— honor another's personal space.

- **Use a firm handshake.**

  A firm handshake conveys confidence. A limp handshake

conveys timidity. A good handshake is solid, firm and brief. Stand and extend your right hand to shake the other person's right hand. If your handshake is too limp, change your hand and wrist position to correct the handshake. If it is too hard, ease up a bit on the strength of the handshake. Develop a solid, firm and brief handshake by practicing.

- **Maintain eye contact.**

  Good eye contact is important. Look a person straight in the eye when asking a question. Maintain eye contact while listening to a response. Do not look at the ground; look away; look beyond the person; or, look to the side of the person when meeting, greeting or socializing.

  Good eye contact does not mean "to stare"—but rather to convey you are listening and are interested in hearing the other person.

- **Listen.**

  Sometimes in a new social setting, we feel nervous and are more concerned about what we "say". It is more important that we listen well—pick up on cues—and respond to the speaker.

- **Smile.**

  A smile indicates you are happy and makes another person feel welcome. If you are comfortable enough to smile, a person will more likely reciprocate with a smile.

- **Adjust your voice inflection.**

  Adjust your voice pitch and tone to the environment. Your voice can be too loud or too soft depending on the situation.

Further, you can express your voice in many different inflections that can convey a range of emotions from anger and disgust to happiness and joy.

• **Stand tall and proud.**

There is only one you and only you can convey that you feel great about yourself.

When standing, keep your posture in check with these five steps:

1. Hold head upright with your chin parallel to the floor. The neck should stretch upward. Do not shorten the back of your neck by holding your chin too high. Do not thrust the head forward from the neck. The vertebrae in the neck should continue upward as an extension of the spine.
2. Place chest and hips in good vertical alignment. The ribcage should feel as though it is lifted off of the hips to lengthen the spine. Always allow for formal and comfortable breathing. Do not allow the chest to fall forward or slouch backward in relation to the hips.
3. Allow for a natural curve of the spine. The pelvis/hips should not be tucked under or stick out backward, but should be held in a midway position.
4. Keep the knees positioned directly between the hips and feet. When the knees bend, the alignment of the hips and feet should remain constant.
5. Place body weight slightly forward in the feet. Your body weight should hit in the middle of the feet, between the heel and the ball of the foot.

Remember, do not slouch!

- **Walk with poise.**

  Poise is synonymous with balance. When walking, your body needs to remain in balance and appear effortless and smooth. Acquire an evenly spaced natural rhythm and gait. It is important that you learn how to walk, stand and sit with ease and dignity

- **Sit up straight.**

  Good posture is good for your self-image and the message that it conveys to others. When sitting, keep your posture in check with these simple seven steps:

  1. Sit up straight with your ears, shoulders and hips in alignment.
  2. Keep both feet on the floor.
  3. Lift your chest.
  4. Let your weight fall on your two sitting bones with your tailbones slightly lifted.
  5. Keep your back flush against the furniture.
  6. Keep your shoulder blades back.
  7. Keep your shoulders low.

  Remember, do not slouch!

- **Sit gracefully.**

  When sitting, sit gracefully and do not "flop" or "drop" onto the chair or couch.

- **Keep your hands at your side.**

  Let your hands fall naturally at the side of your hips. Do not place hands in pockets, behind your back, or cross your arms in front of your body.

- **Exude confidence.**

  When presenting yourself, exude confidence in your appearance, handshake, eye contact, stance, posture, voice and poise. From the moment you walk into a room, you set the tone on how others will interact and respond to you.

LESSON 16

THE SORORITY CONVERSATION

This may seem like one of the most difficult areas for you to master, but with practice it gets easier. Begin practicing now. The sooner you begin practicing these skills the easier it will become to implement them during Recruitment.

- **Introduce yourself.**

    When introducing yourself to a new person, look her in the eye; extend your right hand; shake her right hand; and state your name. If possible, mention something about you. For example, state, "Hello, my name is Jane Cutter and I just moved here from Texas."

    Stand and greet people the first time that you meet them or the first time that you see them on any given day.

    Speak clearly. Do not speak too loudly or too softly.

    Act interested.

    Do not chew gum when meeting someone new.

    Use titles (e.g. Mr., Mrs., Ms., Miss., Dr.) and a last name when addressing someone older until asked to do otherwise. For example, the sorority house mother is Lindsay Spencer.

Refer to the house mother as Ms. Spencer until she states something to the effect of "Please, call me Lindsay."

After meeting someone for the first time, end the conversation by saying "it is nice to meet you", "it is a pleasure to meet you" or "I enjoyed speaking with you."

- **Look at the nametag.**

  Nametags assist in identifying people that you may not know or you may not know well. Nametags provide a perfect icebreaker for you to introduce yourself. You may feel self conscious wearing a nametag, but you must wear one in a conspicuous place.

  Each sorority or the Greek Life Office will prepare your nametag in advance to wear during Recruitment. The name tag will contain easy to read large letters.

  Double-check the spelling of your name for accuracy. If the spelling is incorrect, notify the appropriate person because this information is placed in the computer system when making your sorority selections.

  Nametags allow active sorority members to easily read your name when meeting you. Further, it may assist the active sorority members in reconnecting your name and face when it comes time to document information on the "scorecards".

  When being introduced to others, glance at the nametag so you can read the name while listening to a persons name when she introduces herself. By both hearing the name and looking at the nametag, you are more likely to remember the person's name.

- **Introduce others.**

The basic rules for introducing persons in a business or social situations are as follows:

1. *Business Introductions:*

   A person of lower rank is introduced to a higher-ranking person, regardless of gender. With seniority, you get the person introduced to you. For example, the house mother is Ms. Spencer. To introduce your father to your house mother, you say, "Ms. Spencer, I would like to introduce you to meet my father—Quinn McLean. Dad, this is my house mother, Ms. Spencer."

2. *Social Introductions:*

   A male is introduced to a female. A younger person is introduced to an older one. For example, "Mother, may I introduce my girlfriend, Lauren, to you? Lauren, this is my mother, Kathy Hall."

Always introduce people by their full name and title (e.g. Mr., Mrs., Ms. Miss, Dr.). Never introduce people only by their function (e.g. house mother, advisor, teacher, counselor, coach, uncle, aunt). For example, do not say, "Sara this is my house mother." Instead say, "Sara this is my house mother, Ms. Spencer."

When introducing others, it is helpful to mention something about them or their interests. This helps to facilitate a conversation between them.

If you forget someone's name, it is okay to say, "I am terribly sorry I forgot your name." It is better to apologize for forgetting a name than mispronouncing a name or giving a false name. This embarrasses not only yourself, but also the other person.

When you are engaged in a conversation, give it your full attention, even if it is very brief.

Do not spend all of your time with the same group or individual.

Always excuse yourself when you leave a conversation.

• **Give & receive compliments.**

Knowing how to give or receive a compliment is a great way to begin or end a conversation. Compliments are always welcome and appreciated by everyone. It takes only a few seconds to compliment. For example, "Madison, what an awesome outfit"; "Claire, you have the coolest shoes" or, "Allie, you work so hard." Positive comments are nice to receive!

Learn to receive compliments graciously. When someone compliments you, do not deny or refute it. Instead, thank her for the compliment and enjoy the praise. When receiving compliments, say thank you!!! For example, if someone likes your haircut, simply say "thank you." Do not respond, "My haircut is ugly." This response is insulting to the person giving the compliment. Practice saying thank you the next time a person compliments you.

• **Answer & ask questions.**

When answering yes or no questions, clearly respond with the words "yes" or "no". Do not say "yeah", "yep", "nope" or "nah". If the person is older than you, you may want to respond with "yes sir" or "yes ma'am."

Use common sense when asking questions. Do not ask hurtful, personal, or private questions unless your relationship with the person is secure enough to handle sensitive topics. It would hurt your feelings if someone asked you, "How could you have missed knowing that question? It was so easy!" or "How much money did you pay for that shirt?"

• **Listen attentively.**

Do not interrupt a person in the middle of her response. Let the other person finish what she is saying before you ask the next question.

• **Look at the person speaking.**

If you look at the ground, the sky or anywhere else, you convey the message that what the speaker is saying is not important or that you lack self-confidence. Either way, you are not sending a positive message.

• **Ask questions at sorority parties.**

During Recruitment, you have only a small amount of time to make a good impression. Again, you must be yourself. It is best to find common grounds of conversation and avoid controversial topics that could create conflict between you and an active sorority member. It only takes one active member to campaign against you for you to be cut from the sorority house.

Possible questions to ask during Recruitment are as follows:

1. Where are you from? Or, How often do you get to go home?
2. What do you like best about this sorority?
3. What high school did you attend?

4. What volunteer work do the sorority members perform?
5. Does the house have a study area? Exercise area?
6. What is required of a New Member / Pledge?
7. Do actives and New Members attend all events?
8. What types of activities have you been involved in?
9. What is the sorority's philanthropy?
10. What is your major?
11. What other sororities and fraternities do you have social events with? Sit at football games with? etc.
12. What size is the New Member / Pledge class?
13. Do you take Freshmen, Sophomores, and Juniors in the New Member / Pledge class?
14. What is your "live in"/"live out" policy? Are all seniors able to "live out" of the sorority house?
15. What is your house mother like?
16. What are your meal hours? Do you have meal service on Sunday nights?
17. Do you have a laundry facility in the sorority house?
18. What are the social obligations?
19. What are the financial obligations?
20. Do you have a spring and fall formal?
21. What is the sorority house's GPA?
22. Do you have New Member / Pledge moms and Big Sisters?
23. Is it possible to maintain part-time employment, attend college, and fulfill my commitment to the sorority?
24. Do you have family weekends?
25. Do you have single, double, triple or dormer rooms?
26. What are the rules pertaining to living in the sorority house?
27. What is the parking like at the sorority? Are you allowed to have a car if you live in the sorority house?
28. What classes are you taking this term?
29. Are there any classes/professors that you can recommend?

30. Where is your favorite place to study?
31. Where is your favorite place to eat pizza? Mexican food? Italian food? Chinese food? etc.
32. Does the sorority offer need based scholarships or other payment plans?
33. What is your visitor policy?
34. Do you change roommates/rooms mid-year or do you have the same roommate/room all year?
35. Where do the sorority members live during the summer if they are taking courses at the college?
36. What aspects of the sorority encouraged you to join?
37. What other organizations have you been involved with as a result of your sorority membership?
38. Do sorority alumnae come back to visit the sorority each year? Do you have a lot of alumnae support? Do you have an alumnae newsletter?
39. Do you have a homecoming weekend? Dads' weekend? Moms' weekend? Greek Week? etc.
40. What did you do last summer? Or, if it is a winter Recruitment, "What did you do over winter break? What are yours plans for spring break?
41. How long is the New Member/Pledge program? How much time is needed to devote to it?

The above questions keep the conversation flowing. If you are inspired, think of some original questions of your own! Most importantly, do not ask questions that do not reflect your personality or interests.

Specifically, if it is unimportant to you whether or not the sorority offers scholarships, then do not ask about it. Your question will come across as insincere and you probably will appear bored when you are given a response.

During Recruitment, you must find common grounds of conversation!

- **Do not offend sorority girls.**

When attending sorority parties, do not offend any of its members. It only takes one active member to have you "cut" (also known as "eliminated") from being invited back to the sorority. Therefore, the following is a list of Don'ts:

1. Do not ask questions that the sorority members are not able to answer—(e.g. questions regarding initiation, rituals, handshakes, secret code words). The sorority initiation process and rituals are kept secret until the New Member / Pledge is initiated into the sorority house and will not be revealed until then.
2. Do not discuss controversial topics that could offend an individual. These topics include, but are not limited to, politics, religion, and abortion.
3. Do not act bored.
4. Do not act like you are "too good" to join a particular sorority. Not only is this disrespectful, but highly offensive for the active sorority members.
5. Do not spend too much time talking to any one active sorority member. It is the entire sorority that votes and people will not vote for someone they do not know.
6. Do not talk badly or gossip about other sororities. The person you are talking to may have a sister, best friend, or study partner in another sorority and this information will get back to the other sorority.
7. Do not talk badly about other Potential New Members / Pledges.
8. Do not go back to sororities that you have no interest in joining. It is a waste of your time and the sorority member's time.
9. Do not over-talk—listen with interest and ask questions.
10. Do not complain.

11. Do not brag about yourself, your family, or your connections.
12. Do not be a "know-it-all".
13. Do not seek only to charm and entertain. Let your charm and humor shine through without forcing it!
14. Do not re-invent yourself during Recruitment. Be yourself.
15. Do not make decisions about a sorority based on someone else's opinion.

Lesson 17

College Etiquette & Technology

During Recruitment and during your New Member Period, you will receive telephone calls and emails from your Recruitment Counselor and sorority sisters. Likewise, if you have a roommate, she may be receive similar telephone calls and emails. It is always best to use professional telephone and email skills and to act with diplomacy.

- **Telephone**

    1. *Answering the Telephone*

        When answering a telephone have a "smile" in your voice and state "hello" instead of "yeah." Discuss with your roommates, how each of you should answer the telephone? (e.g. "Hello" or "Hello this Emily and Natasha's room). Even if you have Caller ID and think it is your friend calling, you should still follow the same protocol because you never know who could be calling from someone else's telephone.

        When receiving a telephone call for a roommate, do not yell, "pick up the phone" or "it's for you". If you yell, you are yelling into the caller's ear. Simply, locate the roommate and advise her of the telephone call. Likewise, you need to ask your roommate to follow the same courtesy for you.

If a caller asks for someone that is either not home or busy doing something else, always respond that the person is busy or unavailable. For example, someone calls for your roommate, Gracie, but Gracie is at the mall. Respond to the caller, "I am sorry, but Gracie is not available at the moment. May, I take a message and have her call you back?" Or, a person calls for your roommate while she is in the bathroom. Simply state, "I am sorry, but Gracie is unable to come to the telephone. May I take a message and have her call you back?"

When talking on the telephone, do not eat, drink or chew gum. Not only is this rude, but also it makes it difficult for the caller to understand your words.

2. *Making the Telephone Call*

When making a telephone call, have a "smile" in your voice, speak clearly, state hello and indicate your name and reason for calling. For example state, "Hello, my name is Lindsay and I am calling to speak with Alayna." Do not state, "Is Alayna home?" This is not only inappropriate, but also rude to the person answering the telephone by not greeting them with a "hello" or "hi".

Always end conversations by saying "good-bye." Just because you know you have finished your conversation, it does not mean the other person is aware that the conversation has ended.

- **Leaving Messages**

1. *Leaving messages with a Person*

When leaving messages with another person, have a

smile in your voice and ask the other person if they are willing to take a message for you. Speak clearly and give the person your name, telephone number and reason why you are calling.

For example state, "Hello, this is Spencer Hall and I am calling to speak with Quinn Cutter. We are in the same Economics course and I have questions regarding our homework assignment. Can you please ask Quinn to call me back at telephone number xxx/xxx-xxxx. Thank you. Have a nice evening! Good bye."

2. *Leaving messages via Voicemail—*

When leaving messages via voicemail, have a smile in your voice, speak clearly, speak slowly, and give the person your full name, date, time, telephone number and reason for the call. For example, state, "Hello, this is Spencer Hall and I am calling to speak with Quinn Cutter regarding our Economics homework. It is 8 p.m. on Wednesday. I will be up until 11 p.m. Please have him call me back at xxx/xxx-xxxx. Thank you. Good bye." Remember to keep your message concise and brief. Also, do not speak too quickly as the person on the receiving may need to write down key information. It is good practice to repeat your name and telephone number twice when leaving voicemail.

- **Taking Messages**

  1. *Taking Messages from a Caller*

     When taking messages from a caller, ask for the caller's name, telephone number and reason for calling. Do not ask, "Why are you calling." Instead ask, "May I tell her why you are calling?" [As a safety reminder— if you do not know the person, do not divulge that you are alone!] Further, when writing your message for another roommate, write it legibly with the date and time of the telephone call. Place the telephone message in a location where your roommate will see it.

2. *Taking Messages from Voicemail*

When taking messages from voicemail write legibly and write down everything the caller stated. Do not delete the message unless you are sure you have written all of the pertinent information onto a piece of paper and written it legibly.

• **Email**

When using email, know the recipient of the email address. Even though email is considered an "informal" method of communication, you must always compose your messages with respect and in consideration that others may read your email message.

• **Cellular Phone Use**

Always use discretion when using a cellular phone in a social environment. Refrain from answering and placing cellular calls. Only answer a cellular call after excusing yourself from the immediate area. Do not keep your cellular phone on while attending Recruitment parties. Use the same skills and diplomacy that you would use on a landline telephone.

• **Pager Use**

When using a pager, use the same skills and diplomacy that you would use with a landline telephone. Place your pager on vibrate or turn it off, while attending sorority Recruitment.

- **Blackberry/Other handheld PDA Devices—**

Do not check your emails on your Blackberry or use other handheld devices while attending sorority Recruitment. If you have a family emergency and must access your handheld device, advise the sorority so it does not appear that you are being rude and offensive, and excuse yourself from the immediate area.

LESSON 18

SORORITY HOUSE ETIQUETTE

During Recruitment, during your New Member Period and as an active sorority member, you must know proper table etiquette when dining formally and informally.

Learn these 25 Simple Rules of Proper Dining Etiquette *before* you join a sorority:

1. *The 25 Rules*

    *   **Rule 1—The Napkin**

        Open your napkin and spread it on your lap as soon as you sit down at a table. If the meal is a formal dinner, you wait for the host or guest of honor to place her napkin on her lap first.

        If the napkin is small, a luncheon napkin, or a cocktail napkin, open it completely and spread it on your lap. Fold a large napkin in half before placing it on your lap.

        Do not tuck the napkin into your shirtfront unless eating crab or lobster.

        Do not use your napkin as a handkerchief to blow your nose, to wipe your nose, wipe off makeup/lipstick, or use as a face cloth. Your napkin is to dab at the corners of your mouth and may be used to wipe your hands when necessary.

Do not place the napkin on the table when you are eating!

• **Rule 2—When Can I Eat?**

Always wait for everyone to be seated before you begin eating. Once the host or guest of honor begins eating, you may begin eating. If you do not know what utensils to use, take a sip of water and watch what the others are doing.

• **Rule 3—Perfect Posture**

Sit up straight and be comfortable. Posture should be straight, but not stiff. Do not slouch or lean over the plate or bowl. Keep your feet flat on the floor. When you eat, bring the food to your mouth. Do not bend to meet the food half way.

• **Rule 4—No Elbows on the Table**

No elbows or forearms on the table. Wrists may gently lean there. Elbows can remain on the table briefly in an "informal" meal only when there is NO FOOD on the table.

• **Rule 5—Chew with your Mouth Closed**

Chew with your mouth closed and do not speak when you have food in your mouth. Do not slurp, belch, drool, or crunch your food or drink.

• **Rule 6—Remain Seated**

Do not push your plate or bowl away from you when you are finished—Let it remain in front of you until cleared from the table. While eating at a Sorority House, you are not able to leave the table until permission is received from the House Mother.

- **Rule 7—Pass Dishes to the Right**

  Pass all serving dishes to the right. Dishes are presented or served to the guest's left and removed from the right side. Beverage glasses are filled from the guest's right while standing behind and to the right of the guest.

- **Rule 8—Eat like a "Sorority Girl"**

  Do not stab at your food. Sorority Girls use knives, forks, and spoons to cut and eat food when dining.

- **Rule 9—Obtain a Fresh Plate for the Buffet & No Sloppy Eating**

  Dining at a sorority can be via a "sit down" served meal or via a buffet. Remember, if your meal is from a buffet, always obtain a clean plate every time you go through the buffet line. Once you eat from your plate, NEVER bring your plate back to the buffet line. Leave it at the table for it to be cleared. Do not be messy, even when dining casually.

- **Rule 10—Do not Risk your Life to be Polite**

  NEVER take a bite of any foods that you are allergic to in order to be polite.

- **Rule 11—Do not apply Lipstick or Face Powder at the Table**

  Never pick your teeth, apply lipstick, or face powder at the table. Excuse yourself to a private area, such as a restroom.

- **Rule 12—Apologize for Food Mishaps**

  If you spill your food or drink during the meal, clean up as much as possible while being discreet or excuse yourself to the restroom, if needed. Inform the host and apologize to anyone that your mishap may have inconvenienced.

- **Rule 13—Be Kind & Respectful**

Always be kind and respectful at the table.

- **Rule 14—Say Thank You**

At the end of a meal, say you enjoyed the meal and thank the host and/or cook.

- **Rule 15—Excuse yourself from the Table**

When excusing yourself from the table to go to the restroom, place your napkin in the chair seat or chair arm. It is inappropriate to place a soiled/dirty napkin on a table when people are still eating.

When excusing yourself from the table at the end of a meal, place the napkin to the left of your place setting, if the plates have not been cleared. You may place your napkin in the center of your place setting, if all of the plates have been cleared. Do not refold a napkin to its original state or roll the napkin back into a napkin ring.

- **Rule 16—Remove the Clutter**

Remove purses, keys, glasses, hats, pagers and cellular telephones from the dining table. Place cellular telephones and pagers on vibrate.

- **Rule 17—Keep Eating**

Do not eat too fast or too slow.

- **Rule 18—Leave your Hands Alone**

  Do not play with your hair, earrings, fingernails or touch your head while at the table.

- **Rule 19—I can Hear You**

  Do not speak too loudly or too softly at the table.

- **Rule 20—Salt & Pepper Please**

  Pass the salt and pepper together or pass the salt only and inquire if the guest would also like the pepper passed.

- **Rule 21—Hats Off**

  Do not wear hats to a dining table unless it is for religious purposes or a sorority luncheon or tea.

- **Rule 22—Do not Ruin my Appetite**

  Engage in appropriate conversation and stay away from topics that could ruin a guest's appetite.

- **Rule 23—Wait to be Seated**

  Males must stand and assist, if females are sitting down at the table or getting up from the table. A gentleman holds the chair and seats the female on his right. If the seating assignment is such that no one can assist the female to the gentleman's left, the gentleman must assist the female on his left as well.

- **Rule 24—Save some food for the Dishwasher**

  Do not scrape the plate with your fork, wipe your plate with a piece of bread, or lick your utensils. Do not use your fingers to put food onto the fork.

- **Rule 25—Enjoy the Meal**

Enjoy meeting new people and above all enjoy your meal!

2. *The Place Settings*

Now that you have mastered the 25 Simple Rules of Proper Dining Etiquette, you must know the basics of table settings. As a New Member in a sorority, you may be asked to set the table as part of your assignments.

- Generally, the more formal the occasion, the more courses of food are served. Different sets of utensils are used for each course (e.g. salad fork, dinner fork, dinner knife, bread knife, dinner spoon, soup spoon and so on). Some special dishes require special utensils.
- Everyone at the table has a place setting, whether or not they intend to eat.
- Wipe and dust, smudges and water stains off of glasses, plates, and flatware.
- Inspect table clothes, napkins, and placemats to ensure they are presentable.
- Place the flatware in the order it will be used (working from the outside in), with the first utensils to be used placed farthest away from the plate.
- Place flatware evenly on both sides of the plate.
- Place the forks on the left.
- Place the knives and spoons on the right. The knife blade should point toward the plate.
- Place spoons to the right of the knives.
- Remember an easy rule in place settings: "solids to the left and liquids to the right."

- Remember that European and American place settings have developed over centuries and some differences exist from country to country; sorority to sorority; and family to family.
- Impress guests with a perfectly set table.

3. *Informal/Casual/Everyday Place Setting Diagram:*

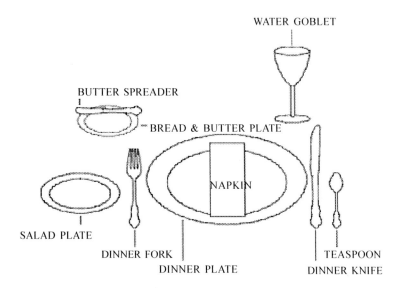

WATER GOBLET

BUTTER SPREADER

BREAD & BUTTER PLATE

NAPKIN

SALAD PLATE

DINNER FORK

DINNER PLATE

TEASPOON

DINNER KNIFE

4. *Steps for Setting an Informal/Everyday/ Casual Dining Table:*

- Determine if you are going to use placemats. Placemats are optional. Placemats are a matter of taste rather than convention. Placemats add color to the table. If you have a fine white linen tablecloth, placemats are unnecessary. If you use placemats, set each placemat one inch from the edge of the table where each guest will be seated.
- Place the dinner plate (the big plate) in the middle of the placemat.
- Place the napkin lengthwise on the left side of the plate (the

crease of the napkin faces the plate) *or* in the center of the plate.
- Place utensils one half-inch away from the plate and from each other.
- Place the fork, tines up (pointy end), on top of the napkin.
- Place the knife, knife blade facing toward plate, to the right.
- Place the spoon parallel and to the right of the knife.
- Place the drinking glass about two inches away from the tip of the knife.

5. *Formal Place Setting Diagram*:

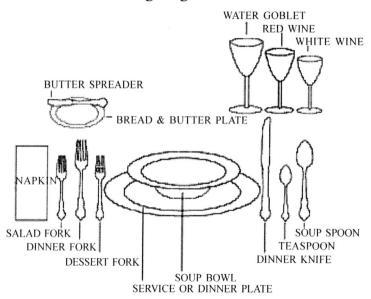

6. *Steps for Setting a Formal American Style Dining Table*:

- Place charger plate in the middle of place setting before the guests are seated. The soup, fish, or salad courses are served on top of the charger plate. It is customary for the charger plate to be removed prior to the serving of the dinner entrée, but may remain during the dinner course if the host chooses. The charger plate must be removed prior to the dessert course.
- Place dinner plate directly on top of charger plate.

- Place a napkin to the left of plate with the folded edge/crease facing toward the plate.
- Place a dinner fork on the left side of plate.
- Place a salad fork to the left of dinner fork. Use a dinner fork/entree fork if your salad is served as the main entree or as a side dish on your main entrée plate.
- Place a fish fork to the left of salad fork.
- Place a dinner knife to the right of dinner plate with the knife blade facing toward the plate.
- Place a dinner spoon to the right of dinner knife.
- Place a soupspoon to the right of dinner spoon, if soup will be served.
- Place a lobster/clam/oyster fork to the right of dinner spoon, if lobster, clam or oysters will be served.
- Place a soup bowl above and to the right of a soupspoon.
- Place the bread plate to the left about two inches above the fork.
- Place a butter knife across the bread plate at a diagonal, upper left to lower right. The blade of the butter knife should face in.
- Place a small salad plate to the left and slightly below the bread plate.
- Place desserts utensils by one of the following three options:

  1. Place a dessert fork and spoon about one inch above the entrée plate. The dessert fork (handle pointing left) is placed above the plate and the spoon (handle pointing right) is placed above the fork.
  2. Place the dessert spoon to the immediate right of the plate.
  3. Place the dessert fork and spoon on the dessert plate along with a finger bowl and presented immediately before the dessert is served. When using a finger bowl, after cleansing your fingers, place the finger bowl and dolly on the upper left side of the place setting. This clears space for the dessert plate.

- Place the largest glass (the water glass/goblet) to the right. It may be filled with water and ice when guests arrive or left empty to be filled at each diner's request.
- Place other beverages to the right and slightly below the water glass.

7. *Can you Recognize & Use all of the Utensils?*

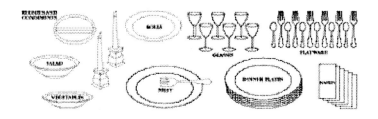

- **Start here**

  When using utensils, start at the far left and far right sides of the plate and work inward toward the plate.

- **Flatware**

  Flatware is also called utensils. Flatware is a set of matching knives, forks and spoons. It is usually silver, but many stainless steel sets and gold plate sets are used.

- **Place setting**

  A space on the table for each guest.

- **Uncommon utensils**

  Small forks are for shrimp, oysters, lobsters and clams.
  Long thin forks are for fondue.
  Lobster claws are for lobsters.

Mallets are to crack open crabs.

- How to Hold Utensils

  Water Tumbler: The water tumbler is held using one hand around it.

  Water Goblet: The goblet is held with the fingers around the stem, and the thumb and index finger on the "bowl" of the glass.

  Holding Flatware: Generally, hold the knife in the right hand and hold the fork in the left hand. Place the utensils on the left and right index fingers and turn them over. Once you lay the knife down, move the fork to the right hand to eat. If you are left handed, make adjustments for ease.

  Cutting food: Keep elbows in toward your body while cutting food to avoid looking like a bird or penguin flapping its wings. Keep the knife behind the fork and hold the food down with the fork tines (pointy part) so food will not slide all over the plate. Do not stab at the food. Use a gentle motion while cutting your food. Cut one piece at a time and not the entire piece of food at once. Lay knife down at the top of the plate after each piece. Do not hold it, lick it, point with it, or lay it down on the table.

- **Eating food**

  Eat food one piece at a time. Chew food completely before swallowing. Chew with your mouth closed. Do not talk with food in your mouth. Do not take a sip of your beverage until after you have swallowed your food (unless you are choking!).

- **Tricky Foods**

Soup & Crackers: Use a soup spoon when having soup. The soupspoon is the utensil placed at the far right of the plate. If the bowl or cup has handles, it is appropriate to drink the soup. Always spoon your soup away from you. In other words, the soup is spooned away from you and then brought back and up to your mouth. Do not blow on your soup. Stir the soup slightly to cool. Do not crumble crackers into your soup. Oyster crackers may be spooned into the bowl. Regular saltine crackers may be eaten along with the soup. When eating soup and getting near the bottom, always tip your bowl away from you to get the last few spoonfuls. When finished, do not leave your soupspoon in your soup cup or bowl. Place the soupspoon on the service place under the cup or bowl.

Bread, Rolls & Butter/Jelly: When served bread or rolls, place a small amount of butter on your butter plate. Tear/break the bread into small pieces and butter each piece separately— one small piece at a time. Do not cut the bread or rolls and do not butter the entire bread or roll, no matter how hard the temptation. If jam or jelly is served, spoon onto your plate and use your own knife to spread onto the roll.

Coffee, Tea & Hot Chocolate: When drinking coffee, tea or hot chocolate and it spills on your saucer, ask for a new saucer.

Appetizers: When appetizers are served using toothpicks. Pick up the appetizer with the toothpick and place on your plate. When ready to eat, use the toothpick as a utensil and place the used toothpick on a plate when the appetizer is consumed. Do not use these toothpicks to pick your teeth.

Grapes: Do not pluck one grape at a time from the stem of a main serving dish. Place a cluster of grapes on your plate and pluck one at a time from your plate. If seeds are inside the grapes, place the grape seed in your hand and place on the plate. Do not swallow or spit the seeds.

Vegetables & Vegetable Dip: Spoon vegetable dips on your plate and dip the vegetables from your plate. Do not stand over the dip bowl and do not double dip.

Brie Cheese: Serve yourself an entire piece of Brie cheese on your plate and cut away at the crust, if desired, on your own plate. Do not cut crust away from the soft part of the main serving dish.

Peas or Corn Kernels: Move fork under the peas and use any available solid food or the side of the plate or knife tip to pick up peas or corn kernels.

Artichokes: Dunk artichoke in butter and scrape it against teeth.

Corn on the Cob: Use corncob holders to avoid butter on your hands.

Spaghetti: Cut up spaghetti, twist fork to roll up spaghetti noodles or use the fork and spoon method by twisting spaghetti in spoon to avoid sucking and slurping.

- **Napkins**

One way to vary table settings is through napkin folding and placement. Two simple, effective techniques are the fan and the triangle.

The Fan: Open a rectangular napkin completely and place flat on the table. Fold the napkin back and forth like a fan. Press down the creases so that the creases are sharp. Fold the rectangle in half and place the center in an empty water glass. Open the two sides of the napkin sticking out of the glass in fan shapes. Set the glass in its original placement or directly in the middle of the dinner plate.

The Triangle: An easy method of napkin folding is to open the napkin flat and fold one corner on top of its opposite corner. Take one of the other corners and fold it over onto is opposite side. Fold the corners on top of the other ones and crease. Take the corner of the resulting triangle, which used to be the center of the napkin, and place in an empty water glass or you can open up the folded triangle and set directly on the dinner plate.

Refresher: Napkins are to be used for wiping the mouth and used for sticky fingers as needed. Do not use it as a "bib" unless you are eating lobster or crab. After completing a meal, carefully place the napkin to the left of your place setting or if the plates have been cleared, place the napkin in the center of your place setting. Do not refold or replace napkin in a napkin ring.

• **Serving Dishes**

Always pass serving dishes to the right (counter-clockwise). Since hosts serve to the right, place the serving platter on your left side to serve yourself. Respect the person sitting to your right by placing the food on your plate and passing the dish without delay.

If you have someone serving you food, dishes are presented or served to the guests left. Plates are removed from the right side. Beverage glasses are filled from the guest's right while standing behind and to the right of the guest.

If you want a serving dish passed to you, ask politely for someone to pass the dish. Do not reach across the table or over someone's place setting to grab the dish.

- **Dining Mishaps**

  If formal arrangements are awkward, try to seat a left-handed guest at the left end of a long table.

  If you have numerous guests and a small table, rearrange each place setting with the utensils grouped more closely together. The most important thing is that each setting looks identical to every other place setting.

  Provide enough food and drink for all invited guests.

  Place flowers where they can be easily seen, but not in danger of being knocked over.

  Remove or relocate furniture to allow for easy movement throughout the space.

  Position food tables for easy access and avoid bottle necks and "dead ends."

  Prepare entertainment and dining details ahead of time.

- **European/Continental Style of Dining**

  The European style of dining is becoming more prevalent in the United States.

  The European table setting differs from the American table setting in that the European style places an additional knife between the entrée knife and entrée spoon. The additional knife is called a salad knife.

  When dining European style, hold the fork and knife with your index fingers in the same manner as the American style of dining. However, the European style does not require you to switch hands after cutting food and does not place the knife in a resting position between bites. Therefore, if you are eating European style, you may cut a piece of food and eat it without putting your knife on your plate.

When taking a break from eating, place the fork and knife in a resting position by crossing the fork over the knife (i.e. make the letter "x") in the center of the place setting.

When finished eating, place the fork and knife (knife blade facing inward) parallel to one another in the 11:25 or 12:00 o'clock positions.

- **American Style of Dining**

  Hold the fork and knife with the index fingers. After cutting your food, switch hands with your fork and knife and place the knife in a resting position on the right side of the plate so you may take a bite of food with the fork.

  When taking a break from eating, place the fork and knife in a resting position by placing the fork and knife parallel to each other on the right side of the plate.

  When finished eating, place the fork and knife (knife blade facing inward) parallel to one another in the 11:25 or 12:00 o'clock positions.

LESSON 19

SORORITY EVENTS

- **Invitations**

  You will receive invitations to parties and functions during Recruitment, during your New Member Period and once you join a sorority. These invitations will indicate who is giving the party, what the party is for, when the party is scheduled, where the party will be located and the time. Typically, the invitation will include a dress code. If not, you will need to contact the party host to determine the appropriate dress while taking into account the season and time of the party.

  Further, the invitation will provide a RSVP or Regrets only subscript. If the party states to RSVP by a specific date, do not miss the deadline. If the party states, "Regrets only," you do not need to respond if you are attending the event.

  If you are hosting a party, you also must write invitations that contain who, what, where, when, and why. When distributing invitations to a party, follow your sorority policy. In the absence of a sorority policy, mail the guests an invitation, call them by telephone or speak to them privately. Do not discuss your party in front of excluded guests. This is rude and may hurt the excluded guests' feelings.

- **Dress Code**

   Review the Sorority Recruitment Handbook distributed by your college's Greek Life Office. The handbook describes the type of dress required for the different functions. If there is a chance of inclement weather, remember to bring an umbrella and/or coat.

   Even if your Recruitment Handbook advises you to dress casually and comfortably during the Recruitment process, do not wear jeans or tennis shoes (unless specifically told to do so during a round of Recruitment parties).

   Generally, wear the same type of clothes that you would wear to a graduation party, church, synagogue, wedding or other similar event. During the first round of events/parties, some colleges may require everyone to wear a commemorative t-shirt to de-emphasize clothes in an effort to equalize everyone.

   During the last round of parties (the Preference Parties), you may be required to wear something semi-formal. Again, review your college's Recruitment Handbook and dress appropriately.

   Before attending a "non-Recruitment" event, determine the proper dress attire by looking at the invitation, contacting the host, or contacting the proprietor at the event's location.

   Image consultants are available to assist you in choosing colors and clothes that work best for your features and body type. Likewise, personal shoppers are available at most major department stores and often are available free of charge.

- **Parties**

  Acknowledge the host and guest of honor. If you bring a gift, personally congratulate the guest of honor (e.g. Happy Birthday, Congratulations on your Graduation, Congratulations on your Acceptance into the Business School) and either hand the gift directly to her or wait to be told where to place it. If you do not know the host, introduce yourself and indicate your relationship to the guest of honor. For example, state, "Hello, my name is Susan Gundry and I am a friend of the birthday girl! Thank you for inviting me to her birthday party."

  Sometimes gifts will be opened during the party and sometimes they will not. Let the guest of honor enjoy her special day!

  If you are the guest of honor, act graciously when opening gifts. If you receive several of the same gifts or you do not like the gift, indicate how nice it is of the person to have taken the time to bring you a gift or how thoughtful the person is to have given you a gift. Never complain about the gift being not to your taste or a duplicate. It is impolite and hurtful to the gift giver. Appreciate the fact that you have friends that care enough about you to take the time to search for a gift, buy the gift, and bring it to the party for you.

  If you are attending a holiday party and the host has different traditions, customs or beliefs than you, respect the traditions, customs and beliefs and do not criticize or judge the host for being different than your own. Remember, you are a citizen of the world and the world is made up of all kinds of people with all kinds of beliefs.

- **Working the Room**

  Be engaged. Think of the other people in attendance.

Smile. The physical act of smiling has positive psychological effects on you and the people around you.

Listen attentively. Give your full attention. Listen for information that could build your relationship.

Act like a host, even if you are not the host. Circulate and introduce guests to one another as you would in your own home.

- **Receiving Line**

  Some events have a receiving line where the hosts are present near the entrance to meet and greet the guests. The hosts should be present and available to say goodbye to the guests as well.

  Beverages are inappropriate in a receiving line for both the greeter standing in line and the guests being introduced.

- **When & How to Eat**

  Do not begin eating until everyone has been served. The host of a dinner party is the last one served. If the meal is getting cold, the host may state something to the effect of "please begin eating while the food is still warm." This is your cue to begin eating without waiting for everyone to be served.

  It is okay to share food with others that are willing to share when dining out. Always request additional small plates and clean utensils to divide the shared food. Do not eat off of the other person's plate.

  When eating food, cut and eat one small piece at a time. Do not eat too fast or too slow. Try and maintain the same pace as the other guests.

Wait until you have finished chewing and have swallowed your food before taking a sip out of your beverage. If you are choking, forget about manners and etiquette and just take a sip.

- **Thank You Notes**

  A thank you card should always be sent to express your sincere appreciation. Send a thank you card within two weeks of receiving a gift, attending a party or wanting to give thanks for an act of kindness. However, sending a late thank you card is better than not sending one.

  Thank you notes are heartfelt expressions of your appreciation.

  Sign thank you notes with a salutation (e.g. From, Love, Sincerely, Fondly, With Love, Respectfully, Best, or Truly Yours) and your name.

- **Good "Sororityship"**

  Always do your best to support your sorority sisters or New Members.

  Even if you do not agree with your sorority sisters or New Members, encourage everyone to do their best.

  Do not criticize anyone in the sorority. We may not always make the same decisions as someone else, but most people try and do the best that they can.

  Do not brag or boast about how good you are or how good your sorority is.

  Do not make fun of another person or sorority as it reflects poorly on you.

  Be kind and gracious.

LESSON 20

SORORITY COURTESY

Basic common courtesy is essential to extend to other people. You must treat other people the way that you want to be treated.

- Use the words—please, thank you, you are welcome, excuse me, and I am sorry. These words make this world a better place.
- Give sincere compliments.
- Be polite and courteous.
- Help others when possible.
- Do not gossip, spread rumors or talk negatively about other people or sororities. What goes around eventually comes around.
- Do not exclude others because they are not like you or you are not familiar about them.
- Do not point, laugh or whisper about other people.
- Do not tell lies. Lies destroy your credibility and embarrass you when your lies are discovered.
- Tell others you love and appreciate them.
- Be kind and gracious.

LESSON 21

PERSONAL CARE

- **Hair, Skin Complexion, Make-up, Hand & Nail Care**

Feeling good and looking good are important to how you feel about yourself and how others respond to you. Take charge of your appearance by looking and feeling your best.

The most essential beauty tip is skin care. Proper skin care begins with the right cleansing products. Wash your face in the morning and evening. If you experience acne or other dermatological problems that cannot be corrected with over the counter products, contact a dermatologist who can assist you in your skin care regime.

Keep hair washed and styled.

Brush your teeth at least twice a day and floss once per day.

Keep you hands, feet, fingernails, and toenails clean and well manicured.

Wear sunscreen.

Play up your best features—eyes, lips, skin, and hair.

If you wear make-up, visit a department store where they will offer complimentary make-up sessions or make an appointment with a professional make-up artist. You and your make-up specialist can decide what works well with your skin, lifestyle, and skin type (e.g. dry, oily, combination skin). Remember, make-up does not last all day. You may need to freshen up between sorority Recruitment parties.

Wash your face to remove make-up before going to bed.

The most important advice is to feel good about yourself and learn to appreciate your beauty. Look on the positive side and not the negative side in all things.

Be comfortable in your own skin!

- **Perfume**

  Perfume should be applied sparingly. The scent should be subtle and not offensive. Many people have allergies and are affected by the smell of perfume. While attending Recruitment parties, it is best to not wear perfume.

- **Nutrition & Exercise**

  An eating disorder is an unhealthy or abnormal relationship with food. The most common eating disorders are bulimia and anorexia. Studies have found that one in three college women suffer from an eating disorder. Eating disorders afflict people of all races and socioeconomic levels.

  The key to ensuring a safe and healthy attitude toward food and exercise is to follow-up on any warning signs that may indicate an eating disorder. Warning signs include:

  o   Obsessing about food, weight, or exercise
  o   Purging or vomiting food
  o   Using laxatives or diuretics

o   Destructive attitudes about body or weight
o   Using drugs, smoking, or caffeine to control weight
o   Exercising constantly

Exercise: The road to good health starts with proper nutrition, sleep, and physical activity. With good nutrition, sleep, and exercise, you will do well in college, work and other activities.

You can make small changes today for a lifetime of good health. The key is to keep your life balanced. If you exercise too much or exercise too little, your health is at risk. Remember; keep a healthy balance in all things.

Nutrition: What you eat, where you eat, how you eat and why you eat are important to your health. You need to eat a variety of foods and well-balanced meal. To improve your eating habits, try to eat the suggested number of servings from the Food Guide Pyramid (Source: U.S. Department of Agriculture/U.S. Department of Health and Human Services) each day from the following food groups:

Bread, Cereal, Rice & Pasta (6-11 servings per day)
Vegetables (3-5 servings per day)
Fruits (2-4 servings per day)
Milk, Yogurt & Cheese (2-3 servings per day)
Meat, Poultry, Fish, Dry Beans, Eggs, & Nuts (2-3 servings
     per day)
Fats, Oils, & Sweets (use sparingly)

Note: A range of servings is given for each group. The smaller number in the group is for people who consume 1600 calories a day (e.g. inactive women). The larger number is for those who eat about 2800 calories a day (e.g. very active women).

In summary, get moving and eat healthy every day. Eat when your body is telling you it is hungry. If you snack, choose nutritious snacks. Choose vegetables, fruits, grains, cereals, breads, lean meat, poultry, fish, beans, and low fat milk and cheeses. Eat fats, oils, and sweets sparingly. They offer little or no protein, vitamins or minerals.

If you are concerned about you or a friend's eating/exercising habits or you suspect an eating disorder, talk to someone that you trust (e.g. house mother, dorm advisor, parent, friend, doctor, teacher, counselor, or relative).

Being happy and comfortable with who you are and what you look like is good for a healthy body and mind.

- **Secrets of Dressing**

  Use colors that work best for your skin tone, eye color and hair color. What works best for one person may look horrible on another person. Develop your own style.

  Keep your clothes iron/pressed, neat, and clean.

  Use accessories to update and add your own personal style to an outfit.

  Visit an image consultant or ask a friend to assist you in choosing those styles that are most flattering to you. Nevertheless, you must feel good in your own skin. You could have the best outfit in the whole world, but if you do not feel good about yourself it will not matter whether you are wearing a burlap bag or Chanel couture.

LESSON 22

HAZING & PERSONAL SAFETY

Hazing & Personal Safety is the most important topic to discuss when talking about joining a sorority or any other organization.

Hazing is an act of power and control over others. It is not accidental. Hazing can be subtle, harassing, or intentional. Hazing is illegal in most states.

Hazing is defined by *Webster's Ninth New Collegiate Dictionary* as follows: To harass by exacting unnecessary or disagreeable work. b. To harass by banter, ridicule, or criticism. 2: To haze by way of initiation.

Generally, most college campuses have defined hazing and developed policies prohibiting such hazing. This information can be obtained through your college's Internet site or through your college's Greek Life Office. A good rule of thumb is if you would feel uncomfortable doing the activity in front of your parents or grandparents, it is hazing.

Typically, hazing is any activity that subjects a person or others to risks of physical injury, mental distress or personal indignities of a highly offensive nature, whether or not such person has consented to participation in an activity.

If you believe you are being hazed during a particular activity, you probably are. You must leave the activity immediately and contact the police and college officials. Hazing is a criminal offense in most states.

Unfortunately, pledges have died during hazing activities that are described as sorority/fraternity rituals. In short, hazing is a serious offense and at any time you believe you or others are at risk of harm, you or others feel uncomfortable, or you or others are acting in an unusual manner, immediately seek assistance and notify the authorities.

1. Sorority & Fraternity Parties or Other Social Situations

Let me be the first to tell you that joining a sorority does not insulate you from being exposed to alcohol, drugs or eating disorders. Sororities are comprised of individuals that are no different than the people living in your dorm, attending your high school, or living in your hometown.

Just because you have joined the same sorority does not mean that you are all alike. Unfortunately, some sorority members will experiment with drugs, have drug problems, experiment with alcohol, have alcohol problems, have eating disorders, or other self-destructive tendencies. You must always take care of yourself by making decisions that are right for you.

Most sororities, if not all, never allow alcohol in the sorority houses and only will co-sponsor alcohol free events at fraternity houses.

Further, you must take precautions to protect your health and safety. For example, when attending a party that has been advertised as a "dry party" (i.e. no alcohol allowed), assume that someone has spiked the punch. In addition, assume that someone has urinated in the punch. Some members of fraternities may not only spike the punch with grain alcohol, but also may urinate in the punch too.

Moreover, even when you are standing in front of the person giving you your drink—whether it be soda, lemonade, water or any other beverage—keep the drink with you at all times. Yes, that means discarding your drink or taking it with you into the bathroom. The reason for this is that you do not want someone to slip something into your drink (e.g. date rape drug) while you are away.

Unfortunately, we live in an era where we do not walk alone at night, we lock our doors, and now we must monitor our beverages. Last, if you ever believe a friend/sorority sister/new member is acting out of character or unusual, take her to the local emergency room and have a physician monitor her. Tragically, young women have died from unknowingly consuming drugs that had been slipped into their drinks. Your intervention could mean the difference of life and death.

2. *Depression*

Some students may experience depression during their college years. Depression may be caused by an unhappy event or from an unclear cause. Depression must be evaluated, diagnosed and treated by a professional.

If you, or someone you know, is experiencing or exhibiting any of the following symptoms, seek treatment from a licensed physician/ therapist/psychologist/psychiatrist:

- Frequent crying spells;
- Isolating from friends or family;
- Sense of hopelessness, guilt, or self-blame;
- Thoughts or discussions about suicide;
- Little or no joy in life;
- Not taking care of yourself (herself or himself); or,
- Not able to cope with routine events,

A professional must evaluate, diagnose and treat a depressive disorder. Some factors that play a role in depression are diet, illness, drugs, medications, biochemical imbalances, and environment.

3. *Eating Disorders*

An eating disorder is an unhealthy or abnormal relationship with food. The most common eating disorders are bulimia and anorexia. Studies have found that one in three college women suffer from an eating disorder. Eating disorders afflict people of all races and socioeconomic levels.

The key to ensuring a safe and healthy attitude toward food and exercise is to follow-up on any warning signs that may indicate an eating disorder. Warning signs include:

- Obsessing about food, weight, or exercise
- Purging or vomiting food
- Using laxatives or diuretics
- Destructive attitudes about body or weight
- Using drugs, smoking, or caffeine to control weight
- Exercising constantly

If you are concerned about you or a friend's eating/exercising habits or you suspect an eating disorder, talk to someone that you trust (e.g. house mother, dorm advisor, parent, friend, doctor, teacher, counselor, or relative).

Organizations are available to help you (or someone you know) to receive assistance for an eating disorder. The organizations are as follows:

1. National Association of Anorexia Nervosa and Associated Disorders
    Visit its Internet website at *www.anad.org* or call 1-847-831-3438.

2. National Eating Disorders Association
    Visit its Internet website at *ww.nationaleatingdisorder.org* or call 1-800-931-2237.

3. Anorexia Nervosa & Related Eating Disorders, Inc. Visit its Internet website at *www.anred.com*.

4. Support, Concern and Resources for Eating Disorders ("S.C.a.R.E.D.")

Visit its Internet website at *www.eating-disorder.org* and locate organizations located in your area.

[*See* "Lesson 21: Personal Care" in this Handbook].

5. *Substance Abuse*

Substance abuse is defined as excessive or illegal use of alcohol or drugs, including using drugs without medical justification. As a college student, you will be exposed to alcohol and drug use.

Unfortunately, binge drinkers, drinking to get drunk, illegal drug use, and abusing drugs contribute to campus crimes, academic problems, and student injuries.

If you, or someone you know, suffers or experiences any of the following warning signs, you must seek help from a professional:

- Experiencing hangovers
- Experiencing blackouts; not remembering events
- Having unprotected and unplanned sex
- Experiencing school problems
- Receiving poor grades
- Missing class because of alcohol or drug use
- Participating in embarrassing or dangerous activities
- Requiring medical or police intervention as a result of ingesting substances
- Withdrawing / isolating from family and friends

6. Sexual Abuse

Tragically, many college women will experience sexual aggression by coercion, threats, or violence. The aggressor can be a friend, date, relative, neighbor, spouse, or stranger.

Sexual abuse is defined as non-consensual touching. Any intentional touching of sexual private body areas to humiliate, degrade, or sexually arose one of the participants is considered sexual abuse.

In order to deter sexual abuse, you must set sexual boundaries and use the buddy system. Never walk alone in the dark. Common sense is your best protection against crimes. Always be aware of your surroundings. Plan in advance to coordinate times with friends to walk to the library, campus housing, your car etc. when it is nighttime. Always call campus security, if you are forced to walk somewhere alone.

Further, notify someone of all of the details of who you are going out with on a date (e.g. name of person that you are going to meet; where the person lives; telephone numbers; where you will be going; and when you will be returning.)

Advise someone to follow-up on your whereabouts if you do not arrive back at the scheduled time.

Contact the police and campus security if you think a crime has occurred.

7. Information & Programs Available

National sorority organizations maintain comprehensive libraries of programs and information for women's personal and professional development. Contact the national sorority organization to learn more about information and programs on drugs, alcohol, eating disorders, depression, rape, sexual harassment, and safety programs. Further, national organizations have programs that educate members about management, finances, and leadership skills.

LESSON 23

LET'S TALK TO THE PARENTS

You may experience difficulties transitioning from high school to college. You may experience a whole range of emotions from excitement, anxiety, anticipation and sadness. You are leaving your home, friends, and family to begin a new journey in life.

Sororities can be helpful in making this transition easier on you. Sororities can provide a home away from home. Conversely, if you do not get invited to join a sorority, the transition to college may seem even more difficult and create additional emotions of disappointment, disbelief, and anger.

Although sororities can provide you with lifelong opportunities of friendship, career networking, leadership, and the ability to serve your community, you can find other ways to reach these goals while attending college other than joining a sorority.

If at any time, you are homesick, disappointed, or discouraged about the Recruitment Process or any of your college experiences, talk to your parents. You may be surprised to learn that they are also experiencing a wide range of emotions in adjusting to a daughter leaving the nest.

Good luck and enjoy your college days!

LESSON 24

FINAL EXAM

Are you the ultimate sorority girl? Take this final exam to see if you have want it takes to be the ultimate sorority girl!

1. When you visit your college campus, do you dream about?
   a. Attending your classes
   b. Meeting new friends
   c. Meeting fraternity boys
   d. All of the above

2. What concerns you most about college?
   a. Finding your way to the library
   b. Attending an 8:00 a.m. class
   c. Having a roommate that annoys you
   d. Not becoming a member of a sorority

3. At the end of your high school day, you spent your afternoons?
   a. Watching television or sleeping
   b. Participating in school clubs
   c. Pet Sitting
   d. Socializing, volunteering, working, and attending sporting events

4. During high school, you?
   a. Talked on the telephone constantly

   b. Shopped at the mall for the latest fashionable outfits

   c. Studied for your tests, ACTs, and SATs

   d. Turned in all of your homework assignments, attending student council events, attended sport practice, organized a fundraiser for a worthy cause, held a part-time job, kept informed on the latest gossip, cleaned your room and donated your time to tutor underprivileged kids or talk to the elderly.

5. When following rules, you tend to?

   a. Follow the rules only when it is convenient for you

   b. Follow the rules if the mood strikes you

   c. Not follow the rules

   d. Always follow the rules; and if for some reason you cannot, you advise someone of your limitations.

6. The primary reason you are going to college is because?

   a. Your parents told you that you had to

   b. You had nothing better to do

   c. You can visit your boyfriend without parental supervision

   d. You have "big dreams" of contributing to the world

7. When you see a sorority house you?

   a. Have a vague idea of what it is

   b. You think you want to visit it someday

   c. You have no reaction

   d. You want to join one (and soon!)

8. When you graduate from college, you see yourself?

   a. Leading a company/Law firm/Accounting Firm

   b. Discovering a medical breakthrough or joining the Peace Corp

   c. Starting a family

   d. Any, or All, of the above

Answer Key

If you answered all D's—You are the "Ultimate Sorority Girl"! You have lived your life to prepare for the moment of joining a sorority.

If you answered any A's, B's, or C's—You have what it takes to be a sorority girl—there is not any one type. You need to decide if you have the time, energy, and finances to join a sorority while maintaining your individual style!

LESSON 25

TRIVIA: FAMOUS GREEKS

Many famous entertainers, athletes, entrepreneurs, politicians, writers, artists, musicians, journalists, comedians, Supreme Court justices and others have participated in sororities and fraternities. Just to name a few:

> John Adams—Maya Angelou—Kirstie Alley—Neil Armstrong—Ruth Bader-Ginsberg—Candice Bergen—Ingrid Bergman—William Brennan—Dr. Joyce Brothers—Pearl Buck—Jimmy Buffet—Carol Burnett—George Bush—Dixie Carter—Wilt Chamberlain—Bill Cosby—Calvin Coolidge—Rita Coolidge—Kevin Costner—Katie Couric—Cheryl Crow—Elizabeth Dole—Julie Louis-Dreyfuss—Faye Dunaway—Dwight D. Eisenhower—Michael Eisner—John Elway—Farrah Fawcett—Geraldine Ferraro—Roberta Flack—Malcom Forbes—Gerald Ford—Faith Ford—Harrison Ford—Henry Ford II—Robert Frost—Art Garfunkel—Zina Garrison—Lou Gehrig—Phyllis George—Leeza Gibbons—Amy Grant—Horace Grant—Warren G. Harding—Goldie Hawn—Florence Henderson—Orel Hirshiser—Lena Horne—Kay Bailey Hutchinson—Lee Iacocca—Jesse Jackson—Kate Jackson—Thomas Jefferson—Star Jones—Michael Jordan—Ashley Judd—Nancy Kassenbaum—John F. Kennedy—Carol Lawrence—Joan Lunden—Martin Luther

King, Jr.—Patti LaBelle—Harper Lee—David
Letterman—Ann Margaret—Thurgood Marshall—
Matthew McConaughey—Bette Midler—Paul
Newman—Jack Nicklaus—Deborah Norville—
Sandra Day O'Connor—Georgia O'Keaffe—Sarah
Jessica Parker—Jane Pauley—James Polk—Marilyn
Quayle-—Rosa   Parks—Elvis   Presley—Jada
Pinkett—Brad   Pitt—Gilda   Radner—Ronald
Regan—Joan Rivers—Orville Redenbacker—
Franklin D. Roosevelet—Theodore Roosevelt—Carol
Keeton Rylander—Wally Schirrs—Pat Schroeder—
Mike Schmidt—David Schwimmer—Gail Sheehay—
Mark Spitz—Dinah Shore—Anne River Siddons—
Carly Simon—Paul Simon—Dr. Benjamin Spock—
Dr. Seuss—Julia Sweeney—William Howard Taft—
Marlo Thomas—Harry Truman—Peter Ueberroth—
Kurt Vonnegut—Sela Ward—Maxine Waters—
Dionne   Warwick—Tom   Watson—Kimberly
Williams—Woodrow Wilson—Joanne Woodward.

-ABOUT THE AUTHOR-

Kirsten McLean, J.D., M.B.A. lives in the San Francisco Bay Area. She received her Bachelor of Arts in Economics from the University of Michigan, Master in Business Administration and Doctorate of Jurisprudence from the University of Houston.

During college, Kirsten was an active sorority member of Chi Omega and served on college Panhellenic advisory committees. After college, she was an active member in the Chi Omega Alumnae organization, the Junior League of Houston and the Junior League of Palo Alto.

Printed in the United States
32153LVS00006B/30

9 781413 440942